Highland Railway:
People and Places

Highland Railway: People and Places

FROM THE INVERNESS AND NAIRN RAILWAY TO SCOTRAIL

BY NEIL T. SINCLAIR

breedon books
PUBLISHING

First published in Great Britain in 2005 by
The Breedon Books Publishing Company Limited
Breedon House, 3 The Parker Centre,
Derby, DE21 4SZ.

For Bert Campbell and Willie Duncan

ISBN 1 85983 453 1

Printed and bound by CPI Group, Bath Press, Lower Bristol Road, Bath, Avon, BA2 3BL.

Contents

Acknowledgements

I have been able to write this book because of the information given to me by many people since the late 1950s when I made notes of the reminiscences of railway workers at Lochgorm Works and Culloden Moor station. I also learned of some of the Highland Railway chief officers from my father who had been at Inverness Royal Academy with their sons and daughters in the 1900s.

I have been fortunate to be able to gather many more reminiscences from staff and retired staff in recent years. I am particularly grateful to Bert Campbell and Willie Duncan, and also to Callum Gault, Willie Gault, Jock Hay and Willie Wilkie. Thanks are due to Alan Dougall, Derek Mackintosh and John Yellowlees of First ScotRail for providing information on railways in the Highlands today.

The chapters about the two major Highland Railway civil engineering families have been greatly helped by information I have been given by Anne-Mary Wharton (née Paterson) and Hamish Roberts. David Stirling has shared with me his knowledge of railway staff and operations as well as commenting on the text. I am most grateful to them and also to my wife Helen and Ian Carr who read through the manuscript and made helpful suggestions.

The book has benefited greatly from the help given by the Highland Railway Society, several of whose members are mentioned above, and from articles published in the Society's quarterly *Journal*. I would warmly recommend membership of the Highland Railway Society to all who are interested in the HR. The membership secretary is: John Fairlie, Winter Field, Terrys Lane, Cookham, Berks, SL6 9TJ and their website is: www.hrsoc.org.uk.

I have carried out much of the research for *Highland Railway: People and Places* in Inverness and my thanks are due to the staff of the Highland Council Archives and Inverness Reference Library for their assistance.

Several of the people mentioned above have greatly helped in providing photographs for the book, as have the Highland Railway Society, Michael Blakemore, Richard Casserley, Howard Geddes, Hamish Stevenson and Peter Tatlow.

Illustration Credits

Atholl Country Life Museum: 63. Author: 26, 36, 78 lower, 111 lower right, 113, 115 lower, 117 bottom, 124, 130 lower, 134-5, 140 lower, 141-2, 153 right. British Railways Board: 17 lower, 81 upper, 151, 153 left. D. Burton (Highland Railway Society Collection) 77. Bert Campbell: 14 upper, 82, 87, 89, 95, 96 , 99 –102, 105, 110 upper, 11 lower left. Ian S. Carr: 25. H.C. Casserley 21 upper, 74, 119 lower, 120. R.A. Dale: 43, 42 lower, 44, 49-50, 68, 72. Willie Duncan: 66, 67 upper, 68, 76, 78 upper. A.G. Ellis 110. Willie Gault 10, 11 upper, 17 upper, 20, 94, 114 lower, 115 upper, 116, 117 top and middle, 122 upper, 140 upper, 147. A.E. Glen 122. Jock Hay: 121. Highland Council Archives: 57 upper, 58, 60, 146. Highland Photographic Archive: 40 upper, 69, 129 upper. Highland Railway Society: 51 lower, 54, 55, 126, 136. Douglas Hume: 123. D.L.G. Hunter (J.L. Stevenson Collection): 23, 75. Inverness Museum and Art Gallery: 128. David Lawrence: 108. LCGB/Ken Nunn Collection: 21 lower, 119 upper. Neil Mackay: 81 lower. Willie Peddie: 132 right, 138 uper, 139. Pendragon Collection: 43 upper, 47, 52, 71 lower, 73, 107 upper, 143-4, 150. Hamish Roberts: 40 lower, 41. Hamish Roberts (Highland Railway Society Collection): 11 lower, 33, 37. Scottish Railway Preservation Society: 9, 18-9, 57 lower. Ian Scrimgeour: 29 lower, 110 lower, 118, 157-9. W.S. Sellar: 137. Hamish Stevenson: 80. J.L. Stevenson: 14 lower, 61-2, 79, 107, 109, 129 lower, 131, 132 left, 133 top. Strathspey Railway: 38 upper. Peter Tatlow: 38 lower, 71 upper, 130 upper. W.E.C. Watkinson: 24, 154-6. Anne-Mary Wharton, 27-8, 46. Gavin Wilson (Author's Collection): 35 lower, 160 lower, 161 upper. Gavin Wilson (Pendragon Collection) 15 lower, 160 upper, 161 lower, 162 upper. Gavin Wilson (Peter Tatlow Collection) 162 lower. The upper picture on p111 is given with the kind permission of Aberdeen Journals Ltd. The remaining illustrations are from the Author's Collection.

Introduction

This book looks at some of the people associated with the railways of the Highlands over 150 years. It concentrates on specific individuals who spent their working lives in engineering, maintaining and operating the Highland Railway system, sometimes under appalling weather conditions. It also outlines how the railway changed some of the towns it served and how it created new communities along its route. The last two chapters look at a few of the railway enthusiasts who have ensured that the memories of the Highland Railway still live on, more than 80 years after the company disappeared.

Highland Railway: People and Places is not a history of the company or its staff. There have been several good books written on the company, its individual lines and its locomotives. They have covered the directors, general managers, locomotive superintendents and Joseph Mitchell, the pioneering railway engineer in the region. Little has, however, been written about the rest of the HR staff, apart from a few recent articles in the *Highland Railway Journal*.

The information on the HR staff in the Victorian and Edwardian periods has been taken from documents in the Highland Council Archives, contemporary newspaper reports and the minute books and other records of the Highland Railway in the National Archives of Scotland. From the 1910s onward I have been able to draw on the memories of those who worked on the railways.

Many people have helped to make this book possible, as noted in the acknowledgements, but there are two who have made outstanding contributions. Bert Campbell has shared with me his reminiscences, which extend back 90 years to the time when he was growing up in his father's stationmaster's house at Lairg. Willie Duncan has provided valuable information about the permanent way staff from the time he became a lengthman in 1931.

I hope *Highland Railway: People and Places* will provide a deserved record of the achievements of Bert Campbell, Willie Duncan and all the other 'unsung heroes' who have worked on the railways of the Highlands.

Neil Sinclair
Sunderland
April 2005

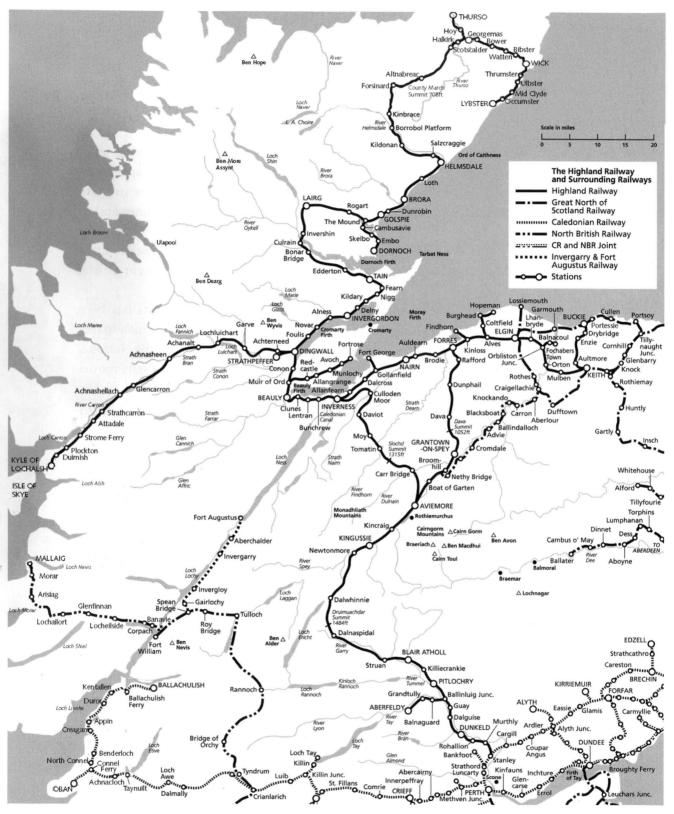

The Highland Railway.

CHAPTER 1

The Railway and its Staff 1855–2005

The official opening of the Inverness & Nairn Railway (I&NR) on 5 November 1855 was one of the most significant events in the history of the Highlands. The development of the railway system changed the economy of the region and transformed, and indeed created, communities along its routes. It also led to the Highland Railway (HR), formed in 1865, becoming the largest single employer in the region. In 1921 it employed 3,490 people.

A Highland Railway family outside the station house at Conon in 1912. James Morrison (centre), the stationmaster, who came from Wester Ross, had joined the HR as a clerk at Dalcross in 1893. He had worked at several stations including Murthly where he met his wife Jeannie, who was a dressmaker. From left to right are Iain, James's older son who followed him on to the railway, Jeannie, James, Jeannie's mother, Christine Ballantine, and his other son, Graham. James and Iain appear in later photographs in this chapter.

A wide area of Northern Scotland was served by the Highland Railway. Its main line ran over the Grampians from Perth to Inverness. From here there were routes east to Keith (where it joined the Great North of Scotland Railway's line to Aberdeen), west to Kyle of Lochalsh and north to Wick and Thurso. There were branches to towns off the four major routes. The map on the opposite page shows the full extent of the Highland system.

Letter to Alexander MacDonald, Highland Railway Accountant, from John Campbell, saying that he wishes to take a day off because of his sister's death; rather sadly it was written on Christmas Day. The content of the letter, written at a time when bereavement leave was in the distant future, and the signature 'Your Old Servant' are a reminder that in 1905 Highland Railway staff worked in a very different environment from today.

Downie,
Edderton.

A. MacDonald Esqre.
Accountant.

Dear Sir,

I regret to inform you I will be unable to attend duty on Tuesday, owing to the death of my sister. I, however hope to be on duty Wednesday morning. Trusting you can see your way to allow me off till then.

Your Obd Servant

25/12/05   John Campbell

The Highland Railway, like the other railways in Britain, divided its staff into officers and servants, reflecting Victorian views of society. The officers were the head office officials, based in the head office in Inverness, and the servants were the majority of the railway staff. There was also a distinction between the salaried staff, including station-masters and clerks, who were paid an annual salary, and the waged staff who were paid by the hour. This distinction was reinforced with the rise of the trade unions from the 1900s when the waged staff became members of the Amalgamated Society of Railway Servants (from 1913 the National Union of Railwaymen) or, in the case of some locomotive crews, of the Associated Society of Locomotive Engineers and Firemen. The salaried staff mainly became members of the Railway Clerks Association which became the Transport Salaried Staff Association in 1951.

Some staff changed from being waged to salaried as they moved up the scale to become locomotive or permanent way inspectors. Perhaps the most notable case of progression up the company was that of Thomas Robertson, who started his career as a porter at Ballinluig and became superintendent of the line in 1875. In 1890 he went further and became general manager of the Great Northern Railway (Ireland) and, in 1896, chairman of the Irish Board of Works.

The three main departments of the Highland Railway were a) the locomotive section which comprised engine drivers, firemen, and shed and Lochgorm works staff, b) the civil engineer's staff, which included all the permanent way workers, signal fitters and telegraph linesmen and c) the superintendent of the line's (later traffic manager's) staff of stationmaster, clerks, porters and guards. There were other smaller sections; the hotel manager was responsible for the staff of the Station Hotel in Inverness and the

The fireman and driver on 4–4–0 123 *Loch an Dorb* at Forres in the early 1900s. Both men were members of the locomotive department. The guard, and possibly his companion on the ground, would have been part of the staff of the superintendent of the line. The gong on the locomotive's tender was connected to the carriages' communication cord, allowing passengers to signal an emergency.

refreshment rooms, and later also for the hotels the Highland built at Dornoch and Strathpeffer. The accountant and his staff oversaw the company's financial transactions.

When the Inverness & Nairn Railway opened in 1855 several people on its payroll came from outside the region. This was hardly surprising, as few Highlanders had any experience of this new form of transport. Andrew Dougall, the general manager of the I&NR, came from Perth where he had been stationmaster for the Dundee and Perth Railway, and several station staff from Perthshire followed him north. Others, such as those who worked on the track, had either been navvies or were

William Roberts (1821–1896) was one of the station staff who followed Andrew Dougall, the first general manager of the Inverness Railway, north from Perthshire. William had been stationmaster at Crieff on the Scottish Central Railway before becoming stationmaster at Elgin on the Inverness & Aberdeen Junction Railway and then Superintendent of the Line from 1864 to 1875 when he retired due to ill health. His son, also William, became the Highland Railway's engineer-in-chief (see Chapter 2).

recruited locally. Within two or three decades the vast majority of the HR employees had been born in the Highlands and by the 1890s a significant number of sons were beginning to follow their fathers on to the railway, a pattern which has continued ever since.

It is broadly true that more of the senior officials came from outside the region; all the locomotive superintendents did so. There were, however, exceptions. The civil engineers who built the lines in the region were all Highlanders; they were able to transfer their skills from building roads, bridges and harbours to railways.

Working for the Highland Railway was usually a lifelong career. If staff did leave, it tended to be for a non-railway job in the area. Very few moved to posts with other railway companies; it was again the officials who were the exception. Many of the staff who left the Highlands went to another part of the British Empire, particularly Canada, or a country in the British sphere of influence, such as Egypt or South America.

Until World War One the HR workforce was almost entirely male. Women were employed in the refreshment rooms and in the hotels, in the ladies' waiting room at Inverness station and to clean offices, but little else. In the head office it was men who carried out clerical duties and it was only the introduction of typewriters in the 1900s which led to the employment of women there.

Working for the Highland Railway

The Highland Railway appears to have been a reasonably good employer by the standards of its time. However, improvements in matters such as hours of work and pension arrangements often came only after pressure from the employees, particularly after the railway trade unions became active in the Highlands in the late 1900s.

When staff were dismissed it was often for embezzling money or being drunk, or being involved in the cause of an accident. Sometimes the option of moving the culprit to a lesser post under censure was adopted. On the other hand staff could lose their jobs solely because of 'depression of trade'. Some were of course only employed in the busy summer period, although they might be offered other jobs during the winter, as described in Chapter 7.

Many of the staff worked into their 70s because there was no automatic pension in the Victorian period on the HR, as for most of the population. In 1878 the HR board had agreed that senior officials could join the Railway Clearing House Superannuation Fund with the company paying 2½ percent of the annual salaries towards this. Stationmasters also started to make payments to this fund and by the 1890s all new salaried staff were expected to contribute towards their superannuation.

The directors could agree to make retiring allowances to staff. It was often the officials who benefited most from this. In 1896 David Jones, the retiring locomotive superintendent, was given a supplementary pension of £239 in addition to the £261 he was receiving from the superannuation fund. Other grades of staff could also receive retirement allowances, the amount sometimes being linked to the number of years worked. In 1888 it was decided to give George Critchley, the retiring stationmaster from

Inverness, who had 26 years service, a retiring allowance of £26 per year 'during the pleasure of the Board'. Lump sums were also given to staff. In 1905 Mrs Noble, who had retired as a waiting room attendant after 36 years of service, was given a retiring allowance of £36, the equivalent of one year's wages.

Thomas Fyfe, the 'first and most impressive' stationmaster at Aberfeldy, from its opening in 1865 until his retirement in 1899. When he retired the Marquis of Bredalbane, a director and a prominent local landowner, asked for a supplementary pension from the Highland Railway for him in addition to his Railway Clearing House superannuation fund pension.

In the Victorian period staff who were injured and the families of those killed on the railway were often dependent on the goodwill of the directors for financial help. In 1863 the Duke of Sutherland gave his director's fee of £100 to establish the nucleus of a fund to make such goodwill payments. In July 1865 it was agreed to pay £25 to the widow of John Fraser, a guard who had been killed on duty. Other sums paid included £20 to the widow of the stationmaster at Garve in 1877. In 1880 £10 was paid to the widow of D. Fraser, a pointsman who was killed at Blair Atholl.

The Highland Railway encouraged its staff to belong to three nominated friendly societies which paid benefits following accidents, ill health or death. The men made a regular contribution to these organisations, as did the company. In 1897 after the Workmen's Compensation Act was passed the HR had to make payments to injured staff under this; the three friendly societies the company dealt with were told that the company's contribution to them could not be guaranteed in the future.

The payments made to widows of staff killed on duty are a reminder that fatalities at work were more readily accepted than today. In September 1904 an engine fitter was scalded to death by steam and hot water in the Highland Railway shed at Perth. He had only worked for the HR for eight weeks, and although it was stated that he had received full training, letting a new member of staff work unsupervised in such a dangerous environment seems foolhardy today.

One advantage of working for the Highland Railway was the housing it provided for staff in rural areas. The Perth, Kyle and Wick lines ran through sparsely populated country. In these areas the HR had to build houses for their staff and this was the major reason why the HR had more houses per employee than any other British railway. By 1921 the company owned 482 dwellings. The HR also recognised that the provision of company houses was an incentive for staff to remain with the railway.

Rogart station showing the impact of 22 wagons breaking away from the special fish train from Wick on 1 February 1903. George Mackay, the signalman at Rogart, heard the runaway coming and diverted the wagons into a siding. They would otherwise have collided with the Wick to Inverness passenger train waiting in the loop in the station. Three train crew returning to Inverness in the guard's van of the runaway were injured, but miraculously survived. Such accidents were a reminder that railways were a dangerous working environment for the staff.

Slochd crossing in 1950 showing the pair of cottages built by the Highland Railway and which housed permanent way staff at this date. The HR had to provide houses for staff at remote locations such as this.

Passengers boarding a train by ladder at a railway lengthman's cottage at Craig, 2½ miles east of Achnashellach. On Saturday one train each way stopped at locations such as this on the Kyle line to take the wives of railwaymen for their shopping in Dingwall, though this view appears to show visitors departing from the cottage.

Staff social events

The Highland Railway Board, composed mainly of landowners in the 19th century, was a paternalistic organisation. In November 1866 it decided to give £225 a year to an annual servants' festival. John Edgar Campbell recalls in *The Iron Track Through the Highlands* that railwaymen and their friends came from all over the system to this event in Inverness. It was, however, discontinued in the 1890s by Andrew Dougall, the general manager, because of 'rowdyism'. It seems to have been partly replaced by the Highland Railway Passenger Department Festival for that section's employees and families. The second Festival in 1900 included serious and comic songs, recitations and a performance with a skipping rope. Those taking part were mainly the wives and daughters of HR staff. It is unlikely there would have been any 'rowdyism'.

The Highland Railway Literary Society was founded in the 1870s as the Highland Railway Clerk's Literary Society. Its lectures covered subjects such as the Peninsular War. It also had an annual social in Inverness. Here, among others, Andrew Dougall, the general manager and president of the society, entertained the members by singing *When the kye* [cows] *comes hame*.

The locomotive department had an annual excursion, which catered for the staff's families. *The Scottish Highlander* of 21 June 1894 recorded that on the previous Saturday about 1,200 people left for Aberdeen in a train of 30 carriages. They had a pleasant time viewing the sights of the Granite City and the newspaper recorded 'the behaviour of the excursionists was most creditable and no untoward incident falls to be reported'.

The rise of the Trade Unions

Until the 1900s the HR board was able to decide wages and conditions of service independently. It received petitions from groups of staff for improvements in their conditions and sometimes acted on them, but the staff had to accept whatever decision the directors made.

Trade unions had no real power in the Victorian period on the HR. In his railway memoirs *Time Does Transfix* Alfred Forbes wrote that a branch of the Amalgamated Society of Railway Servants (ASRS) had been formed in the Highlands, probably in the early 1890s, and that his father, William, had been elected secretary. Although this was meant to be a secret his father was visited by an official from Inverness and was threatened with dismissal unless he resigned his union position; William Forbes felt he had to agree to do this as he had several small children.

This first attempt to form a union branch on the HR failed, but little more than 10 years later things were changing. The railways in Britain began to accept the increasing importance of the railway trade unions, especially for the companies serving the industrial centres.

In 1907, following threats of a national strike, conciliation boards were set up for different sections of the waged staff, apart from workshop staff. They considered matters relating to the conditions of service of different sections of the staff. The boards had representatives of the company and of the staff, the latter being elected by the members of the different departments – locomotive, civil engineer's and traffic staff. William Whitelaw, the HR chairman, later said that the Highland Railway had set up conciliation boards only because they had to and that they were not necessary on their system. He also strongly opposed the recognition of unions and claimed they only represented a small minority of the staff. Nevertheless, he stated that two-thirds of the conciliation board representatives were 'union men'.

Continuing dissatisfaction with wages and hours led to a strike on several railways, but not on the HR, in 1911. This resulted in the role of the conciliation boards being strengthened and the unions received partial recognition. By now there were several branches of the Amalgamated Society of Railway Servants on the HR who were pressing for shorter hours than the more than 60 hours worked by many staff.

4–6–0 140 *Taymouth Castle* and 4–4–0 62 *Huntingtower* at Inverness locomotive shed in the early 1900s. In the background are the arches leading to the individual lines inside the roundhouse. In 1915 David Fraser, a locomotive driver, was crushed to death against one of the arches when he apparently slipped off the steps below the footplate of an engine moving into the shed. At the subsequent enquiry James Bell, secretary of the National Union of Railwaymen, argued that the clearances were insufficient, but the jury found that the HR was not to blame. The NUR represented its members on safety issues such as this as well as on wages and conditions of service.

Some improvements to conditions were agreed by both sides while others were not. In June 1912 the company and staff representatives on the HR traffic board could not agree about the hours and wages of shunters. This was resolved in November by the decision of the independent chairman, Sheriff Mackenzie, in November 1912.

World War One and the aftermath

The outbreak of World War One brought massive pressures to bear on the Highland Railway, because of the need to work greatly increased traffic to the naval bases in the north. They had to manage this at the same time as losing many of their experienced staff

Male locomotive cleaners on 4–4–0 15 *Ben Loyal* at Forres (above) and female locomotive cleaners on 4–4–0 73 *Snaigow* at Inverness (below), both probably photographed about 1918. After the end of the war the lads would have gradually progressed up the promotion ladder to passed firemen. Those of their female counterparts who remained on the railway would have been moved to carriage cleaning. Female porters were also transferred to carriage cleaning, which was considered one of the few appropriate jobs for women on railways in peacetime.

to the armed forces. Some 25 percent of the Highland workforce of 756 served in the armed forces; 87 were killed. Women were employed in significant numbers to replace the men. The total of female workers rose from 15 to 138 during World War One. At a large meeting of HR employees at Inverness in August 1915, A. Bellamy, NUR president, expressed concern that women were being used as 'cheap labour', a reminder that women were generally paid less than their male counterparts.

The war also meant that it was difficult to sustain some of the improvements to staff conditions which had been won through the conciliation boards. The minutes of the Inverness branch of the National Union of Railwaymen (as the ARSS had become in 1913) recorded goods guard William McGregor leaving Inverness at 9.10am on 19 May. Because of the heavy traffic the train was held in loops and sidings and did not arrive in Perth until 12.40pm the following day. In spite of the fact that he had been on duty for more than 27½ hours, McGregor was ordered to work the 9pm from Perth to Inverness the same night. He refused and returned north as a passenger. The train fare of 9s 10d (about two day's wages) was subsequently deducted from his pay. All the union could do was to award him one day's unemployment pay.

Pay did improve during the war as bonuses were granted to railway staff, reflecting inflation during this period. After 1914 the Highland Railway was under government control exercised through the Railway Executive Committee, so decisions were taken at a national level in negotiations with the trade unions. By 1919 the Highland Railway wage bill was three times what it had been in 1914.

The station staff at Conon in 1920. Seated is James Morrison, the stationmaster. Standing from left to right are John Mackenzie (porter), Iain Morrison (clerk), Simon Mackenzie (porter/pointsman) and John Chalmers (porter/pointsman). Iain, John Morrison's son, is wearing the uniform cap which clerks put on when collecting tickets. The porter/pointsmen operated the signal cabin as well as carrying out porter's duties on the station. John Mackenzie was moved to Struan in 1922 because of staff reductions at Conon.

The question of how much of the wartime bonuses should be consolidated into staff's permanent pay led to a national strike by the National Union of Railwaymen and the Associated Society of Locomotive Engineers and Firemen between 27 September and 5 October 1919. There was almost unanimous support for the strike on the HR, where union membership increased significantly during World War One. On some days no trains ran at all and only a handful ran on the remaining days; one train to Lairg was driven by the manager of the Inverness electricity works. The strike ended in victory for the unions and the agreement laid down standard wage rates for all parts of the country and local and national staff machinery and wages boards.

Improvements in conditions came into force in 1919–20 with the introduction of an eight-hour day and 48-hour week in normal circumstances. The Highland Railway was unhappy with this. Thomas McEwen, the HR's traffic manager, claimed that the traffic at the majority of HR stations was never heavy and that the staff could not be exhausted, as some signalmen were working in their spare time driving bakers' vans and acting as picture house attendants. William Cox, the HR chairman, said in 1922 that the HR was employing 21 extra staff as a result of the eight-hour day. The HR attempted to lessen the financial impact by withdrawing stationmasters from some stations, reducing staff at others and making alterations to signalling.

The LMS and British Railways

In 1923 the Highland Railway became part of the London, Midland & Scottish Railway. One immediate impact on staffing was the disappearance of posts in the HR head office

Iain Morrison, who appeared in the previous photograph at Conon, is shown here, on the right, in his second post as clerk at Bonar Bridge in 1922. In the centre is William McPherson, the stationmaster, and on the left Donald McKenzie, relief clerk. William McPherson was later stationmaster at successively Boat of Garten, Clydebank and Glasgow Central (Low Level), while Donald McKenzie became stationmaster at Larbert, Stirlingshire, and Whitchurch, Shropshire, and Iain Morrison at Greenhill, Stirlingshire. The fact that all three became stationmasters outside the Highlands showed the wider opportunities available for former HR staff after the formation of the LMS.

A broadsheet with the words of a song which marked the retirement of several engine men on reaching the age of 65. The song notes that this was a change brought in by the LMS. One driver, George Reid, was clearly a stalwart of the National Union of Railwaymen and the sheet was sold in aid of the social event for children organised the No.3 (Loco Branch) of the Inverness National Union of Railwaymen.

Composed, Written and Sung by THOMAS GORDON, Engineman, Inverness, at a Social Gathering in the Commercial Hotel, Inverness, on Thursday, 15th November, 1928.

Tune—Twenty Years Ago.

Now comrades dear, we're a' met here, to bid a fond farewell
To quite a number of our mates, men ye a' know quite well;
The L.M.S. fell on bad times, their funds are getting low,
And Derby's domineering men, they say that they must go.

Now, friends, it's rather hard you know that young men such as they,
Should be cut off so soon in life from earning honest pay,
For they're as good as e'er they were, as sure as we're alive ;
Our Highland men are in their prime, when they are " Sixty-five."

Twelve hours a day we used to work, and derg along the line,
And, Oh ! the pay was unca sma', in the days o' Auld Lang Syne,
But one grand change to please us all, we've now an eight hours' day,
And men, like George Reid, we must thank for our increase o' pay.

He's been a great Trade Union man since his career began,
Right manfully he's done his bit to help his fellow-man
And we're a' doonhearted that our comrade's gaun awa',
The best o' luck to dear George Reid is the wish frae ane and a'.

Then a' oor other comrades, their names I'd like to tell,
There's Will Dargavel and Tom Grant, men we a' lo'e right well,
There's Andrew Young and Guthrie too, and Thompson you all know,
And James Macmillan's on the list of men that have to go.

Nae mair they'll climb Druimnachdar Hill, nor drive a Highland train;
Nae mair they'll run to Keith or Kyle, Dingwall, Wick, or Tain ;
Hot bigends win'na trouble them, their sorrows will be o'er ;
So may they a' be spared and well till far ayont four-score.

Now time is swiftly on the wing, right soon we a' maun go,
Not only leave the Railway, but must leave this world, you know,
And when the time comes we must go—to some it will cause pain ;
But may we all meet up aboon where we'll nae part again.

PRICE TWOPENCE

Proceeds in aid of N.U.R. No. 3 (Loco Branch) Children's Social.

J. G. Eccles, Printer, 28 High St., Inverness.

as their duties were transferred to the LMS headquarters in London or the Scottish headquarters in Glasgow. Matters such as negotiations with the trade unions were now dealt with centrally and standard conditions existed for all LMS employees.

Jobs were also lost at Lochgorm Works as repair work was transferred to workshops in the south. The line south of Struan was transferred to the Perth district and ceased to be part of the area controlled from Inverness.

In Scotland the Caledonian Railway was the dominant partner of the LMS and its general manager, Donald Matheson, became the deputy general manager for Scotland. Shortly after the grouping A.C. Smyth of the Caledonian Railway became district traffic superintendent at Inverness. He was not liked by the former Highland Railway staff and there certainly seem to have been cases where he treated individuals harshly. In his memoirs Alfred Forbes says that former Caledonian staff were encouraged to move to the HR system as those now in control felt 'it needed some of the discipline and efficiency of the south'. Some former Caledonian staff did move north, but conversely some of the Highland staff moved to posts on the Caledonian system.

As well as recounting the unhappiness of some Highland staff with the new regime, Alfred Forbes writes of the impact of the general strike of 1926 when the railway staff of all three unions and other workers came out in support of the miners. Alfred, who was the son and grandson of railwaymen, had started work as a clerk at Burghead goods station in 1922. He was a clerk at Orbliston Junction when the strike broke out in May 1926. Having recently become a member of the Railway Clerks Association, he joined the dispute.

Former Highland Railway 4–4–0 LMS 14274 *Strathcarron* at Orbliston Junction with the Fochabers branch train. Alfred Forbes was working here as a clerk when he took part in the 1926 General Strike and was not immediately re-employed. In his memoirs he recounts incurring the wrath of one of the Duke of Richmond and Gordon's daughters by asking for the fare for her dog when she joined the branch train there.

As in 1919, the strike was well supported and Inverness station was picketed. A few trains were run with staff who had not joined the strike and or with non-railwaymen who were volunteers. However, the General Strike ended in defeat for the union movement, with the railwaymen going back to work after 10 days.

Some of the volunteers were employed as permanent staff and not all of the strikers were taken back immediately. Alfred Forbes had to wait three months before being re-engaged. Some years later he was made redundant from his job at Forres station, when

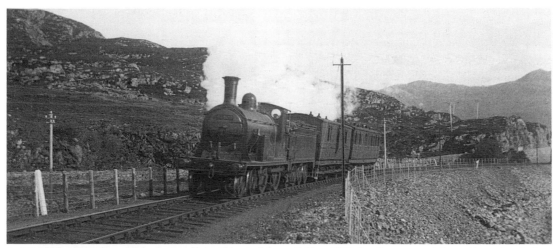

4–4–0 LMS 14409 *Ben Alisky* leaves Kyle of Lochalsh on 7 May 1926, hauling a special working of only two coaches during the General Strike. This suggests that the train was being worked by volunteer non-railwaymen. An account of a journey from Inverness to Perth during the dispute recorded that all the crew were volunteers with the guard changing the points en route.

staff were being reduced, and was told he had to move to London. On protesting that another member of staff was junior to him, Alfred Forbes was told that this was no longer the case as he had lost the time he was on strike. Staff who had remained 'loyal' in 1926 were certainly looked upon more favourably by the railway companies.

By the late 1920s road transport was beginning to take a significant amount of

Page from the register from Moulinearn crossing signal cabin for parts of Sunday 11 and Monday 12 April 1943. They show how heavily used the Highland main line was during World War Two, particularly by goods trains. One of the items in the 'Remarks' column notes that the pouch with one of the single line tablets had been dropped when it was being exchanged. The '213' in the 'Remarks' column indicated that the engine was not fitted with an automatic tablet catcher.

LMS Black Five 4–6–0 5121 on a northbound goods approaching Moulinearn loop in June 1943. 5166 waits with a train in the loop. The signal cabin can just be made out to the right of this engine. It was built in 1942 to control the reinstated passing loop which increased the capacity of the single line between Ballinluig and Pitlochry.

passengers and goods away from the railways. This led to passenger services being withdrawn from the Burghead and Fochabers branches in 1931, with a consequent loss of jobs.

World War Two saw a temporary halt in the decline of traffic and staff in the Highlands. Once again the Highland system was worked to its full capacity and additional crossing loops and signal cabins were built. Women now worked in the signal boxes as well as in some of the same jobs they had done during World War One, as clerks, engine cleaners and porters.

One problem that emerged during the war was that many of the new staff were unused to operating telegraph instruments. This was one reason that the Inverness telegraph office, which controlled the operation of trains over the Highland system, was replaced in 1942 by a control office which was linked to signal boxes by new telephone circuits.

With the nationalisation of railways in 1948 the Highland system became part of the Scottish Region of British Railways. From the early 1950s there was increased competition from road transport. The majority of Highland branch lines closed to passengers between 1943 and 1960; most goods services on these lines had also gone by 1960. This year was also significant as it saw the withdrawal of passenger services from 20 intermediate stations between Inverness and Wick.

The loss of jobs that occurred in 1960 seemed likely to be increased several fold when Dr Beeching's *The Reshaping of British Railways* proposed the closure of all lines north of Inverness as well as the Aberfeldy branch and the original Perth main line from Aviemore to Forres via Grantown-on-Spey. In the event, the lines from Inverness to Wick and Kyle of Lochalsh were reprieved. However, the Grantown-on-Spey and Aberfeldy routes closed to passengers, as did many of the intermediate stations on all the surviving routes in 1964 and 1965. Goods services survived at some of these stations, but generally for only a few years.

Preserved Highland Railway 4–6–0 103 reversing into the yard at Forres in August 1965. The engine was hauling a week-long series of special trains between Inverness and Forres to mark the centenary of the formation of the Highland Railway. Supervising the move from the footplate is locomotive inspector Sandy McBey, who joined the Highland Railway at Burghead in 1917 and retired in 1966. Sandy's grandfather, father and brother also worked on the railways, and all had 50 years of service.

Staff numbers fell after the closures. They were also reduced by the introduction of new equipment. The replacement of steam by diesel traction in 1958–62 meant not only that fewer footplate crew were needed, but also that many of the jobs needed to maintain the steam engines disappeared and engine sheds closed. Similarly more mechanisation was introduced into track maintenance and fewer men looked after longer lengths, while most of the double track sections were singled.

New methods of working meant that even when the railway expanded again there was not necessarily a need for more staff. This was shown when the double track between Blair Atholl and Dalwhinnie was reinstated, along with some loops on the main line, in the late 1970s. The move was to cope with the increased traffic brought by North Sea Oil. The double track and new loops were controlled from only three signal boxes and several other boxes were also brought under their control. As well as the signalling jobs lost here, many more went when radio signalling was introduced on the Kyle of Lochalsh and Wick lines and a new power signal box opened at Inverness in the 1980s.

Station staff also disappeared. The office of stationmaster was abolished in 1965 and area managers were introduced to look after several stations. By the late 1970s there was only one area manager for all the Highland lines. Many other station posts disappeared, with the majority of stations in the Highlands becoming unstaffed and tickets being issued on trains.

47604 *Women's Royal Voluntary Service* arrives at Blair Atholl with an Inverness to Glasgow train in May 1990. The station was then unstaffed, like many on the Highland system. Apart from permanent way and train staff, the signalman at Blair Atholl was the only railway worker on duty between Pitlochry and Kingussie.

In 1982 British Railways was divided into sectors with all the internal passenger services in Scotland becoming part of the ScotRail profit centre of the Regional Railways sector. Further changes came with the privatisation of the railway system in the 1990s which meant that railway staff in the Highlands ended up working for several employers.

ScotRail staff in the Highlands today

In September 2004 I met Alan Dougall, ScotRail manager at Inverness, to find out how the passenger side of the former Highland Railway system was operated and staffed today. The area Alan controls is basically the same as the HR network for the lines to Wick, Kyle of Lochalsh and Keith on the Aberdeen route, but the southern limit is the former Perth-Inverness county boundary, south of Dalwhinnie. The ScotRail franchise was operated by National Express from 1997, but eight weeks after my visit this passed to First Group.

Alan Dougall only deals with the ScotRail passenger operation, the engineering function at Inverness coming under Derek Mackintosh, the depot production engineer, as described in Chapter 8. There are several other companies employing railway staff in the Highlands, with the additional complexity of various companies employing subcontractors to carry out certain work. On ScotRail itself the catering trolley operation is contracted out.

Network Rail is responsible for the track and signalling, but at the time of my visit, track maintenance work was being carried out by First Engineering. English Welsh & Scottish Railways operate most freight services in the area and have a train crew depot at Millburn, Inverness, which provides the locomotives and crews for the goods trains and also the Caledonian Sleeper train. GNER has catering crews based at Inverness with the drivers and conductors for *The Highland Chieftain* coming from Newcastle and Edinburgh.

Nairn station in 2003 with 158735 on an Aberdeen to Inverness service. In today's privatised railway the two staff on duty here have separate employers – ScotRail for station duties and Network Rail for signalling.

Apart from the GNER crews of *The Highland Chieftain*, the railway staff with whom passengers come into contact on the Highland system today are employed by ScotRail and report to Alan Dougall. Eighty-five of the 125 staff are based in Inverness, including 18 of the 36 station staff and 32 of the 40 drivers (four are based at Kyle and four at Wick). Fifteen percent of the employees are women, rising to 50 percent for station staff. Five of the 34 conductors are women. The rise in female employment has been a feature of railways in recent years, extending for the first time to senior management as the managing director of First ScotRail is Mary Dickson.

Dougall is an appropriate name for a railway manager in the Highlands; it was Andrew Dougall who controlled all the railways operating out of Inverness for 40 years from 1855. While Alan Dougall is from an Edinburgh railway family, his wife Shona is from an Inverness railway family. There are still significant numbers of staff with family connections in the Highlands. In addition to the traditional father and son link, today it may well be father and daughter or husband and wife.

As in the past, one feature of railways in the Highlands today is the number of long-serving staff. This distinguishes the area from other parts of ScotRail where there is a higher turnover of staff. Alan Dougall started his own railway career 30 years ago and has worked in the Highlands for 20 years. He estimated that 80 of his 125 staff had more than 20 years experience. Although some might feel a few of the recent changes were not for the better, there was still a pride in working on the railways. The commitment of staff is clearly as important to ScotRail today as it was to the Highland Railway a century and more ago.

CHAPTER 2

Two Civil Engineering Families
The Patersons and the Roberts

In 1839 William Paterson returned to his native Highlands to work for Joseph Mitchell, the region's leading civil engineer. William had been involved in engineering railways in Ireland and the Scottish Lowlands and he was soon involved with surveying the route of the proposed Perth & Inverness Railway, which was presented to Parliament in 1845. Members of the Paterson family were to be involved with the civil engineering of railways in the Highlands for much of the next century.

A second family who played a major role in civil engineering on the HR in the late Victorian and Edwardian period were the Roberts. This chapter looks at both these families. More details about the day-to-day work of civil engineers are given in chapters 3 and 4, which concentrate on two assistant engineers, William Smith and Murdoch MacDonald.

The Paterson brothers and Joseph Mitchell
William, the second son of Donald Paterson, a farmer at Dell of Inshes outside Inverness,

was born in 1812. By 1836, aged only 24, he was working as a civil engineer in Ireland for Sir John McNeil, probably surveying the Dublin & Drogheda Railway. He then returned to Scotland and became involved in the surveying and construction of the Slamannan Railway from the Airdrie area to the Union Canal in West Lothian, before returning north to work for Joseph Mitchell.

Joseph Mitchell was chief inspector for the Highland Roads and Bridges Commission and engineer to the Scottish

William Paterson (1812–1881) assisted Joseph Mitchell in preparing the first scheme for a line between Inverness and Perth submitted to Parliament in 1846. Rather confusingly, there was another William Paterson (no relation) working in railway civil engineering in Scotland at the same time; the other William was the Scottish Central Railway's engineer.

Fisheries Board. He was the visionary who saw the importance of linking Inverness with the south by the direct railway route to Perth, although many doubted its practicality. The Perth & Inverness Railway scheme was put forward to Parliament in 1846, in opposition to the Great North of Scotland Railway, which proposed to link Aberdeen with Inverness. It was, however, the latter that succeeded, the Perth & Inverness being rejected 'on points of engineering difficulties alone'. Joseph Mitchell made reference in his *Reminiscences of My Life in the Highlands* to 'my faithful assistant [William] Paterson (who had worked night and day on our plans)', after recalling how downcast he himself was at the rejection of the scheme.

The Perth to Inverness scheme was revived again in 1853, but it was decided only to seek powers for a line from Inverness to Nairn; this was opened on 5 November 1855. The Inverness & Aberdeen Junction Railway then extended the line to Keith where it met the Great North of Scotland's route to Aberdeen. When this link was completed on 18 August 1858, it was possible to travel by railway from the south to Inverness, but with a change of station at Aberdeen.

The Highlanders continued to work for a direct route from Inverness to Perth over the Grampians and finally achieved this when the Inverness & Perth Junction Railway was completed on 9 September 1863. The Inverness & Ross-shire Railway had meantime reached Dingwall on 11 June 1862, while the extension north to Bonar Bridge was

The bridge over the Spey at Orton on the Inverness & Aberdeen Junction Railway. This was designed by Joseph Mitchell and had the largest single span of any open girder bridge in Scotland. One of the plaques over each end of the bridge, now on display in Inverness station, records that its opening completed railway communication between London and Inverness. Although the line opened in August 1858, the bridge was not completed until February 1859 and passengers had to use the road bridge to cross the Spey for a time.

completed on 1 October 1864. The Sutherland Railway continued the route north to Golspie; the line was opened on 13 April 1868. Branch lines were also built to Burghead in 1862 and Aberfeldy in 1865. The latter was opened when the Highland Railway was about to be formed. It was created by the amalgamation of the Inverness & Perth Junction Railways and the Inverness & Aberdeen Junction Railway, which had previously taken over the Nairn and Ross-shire companies. Joseph Mitchell was the engineer for all these lines.

The Divie viaduct on the Inverness & Perth Junction Railway 10 miles south of Forres. William Paterson supervised its construction and his name appears as engineer on one of the commemorative plaques. The Divie was one of eight viaducts and 126 bridges built over burns and 119 over roads on the line between Dunkeld and Forres which opened in 1863.

Tain station on the section of the Inverness & Ross-shire Railway opened in 1863. This is typical of the stone-built stations with a glazed awning that were built on the lines from Inverness to Keith and Invergordon.

In his railway work Joseph Mitchell was assisted not only by William Paterson, but also by one of William's younger brothers, Murdoch, who had been born in 1826. Murdoch Paterson, who had previously spent two years working in the private office of a bank agent, became articled to Joseph Mitchell for five years in 1846. At the end of this apprenticeship he became the engineer for a firm of contractors who were carrying out major harbour works at Inverness. He rejoined Joseph Mitchell in 1854 to assist in the railway schemes. In 1862, after suffering a stroke, Joseph asked the Paterson brothers to become his partners and the firm of Joseph Mitchell and Company was set up. William left to set up his own business in 1865 and Joseph Mitchell retired in 1868 when his health was failing. Both Paterson brothers were also involved in Joseph's road and other civil engineering work.

Aberfeldy station, which was built in 1865 using material from the short-lived Inverness & Perth Junction Railway station at Rafford. Because of the precarious financial state of the I&PJR all the stations on the Perth line were constructed of wood and some were adapted contractor's huts. Joseph Mitchell and his assistants had little chance to employ the architectural skills they had used on previous lines.

Joseph Mitchell is justly renowned for his major role in planning and engineering railways in the Highlands. Murdoch Paterson is also well remembered, largely because of his significant later work in completing the Highland Railway's main line system. William Paterson, on the other hand, has been treated unkindly by history, with some of his railway work being attributed to his better-known brother.

William Paterson's role in the engineering of railways in the Highlands was certainly of significance. When he came to work for Joseph Mitchell he was the only civil engineer in the Highlands with practical experience of constructing railways. He was the more senior of the brothers during the early period of railway construction. The Inverness & Perth Junction Railway minutes show that he deputised for Joseph Mitchell when the latter was unavailable, as happened when Joseph was recovering from his stroke.

One reason why William Paterson is so little recalled in connection with railways is that after he set up his civil engineering business he mainly concentrated on roads. He became the road surveyor for the Inverness district. There may well have been an agreement about the division of railway and road work with Murdoch. Nevertheless he

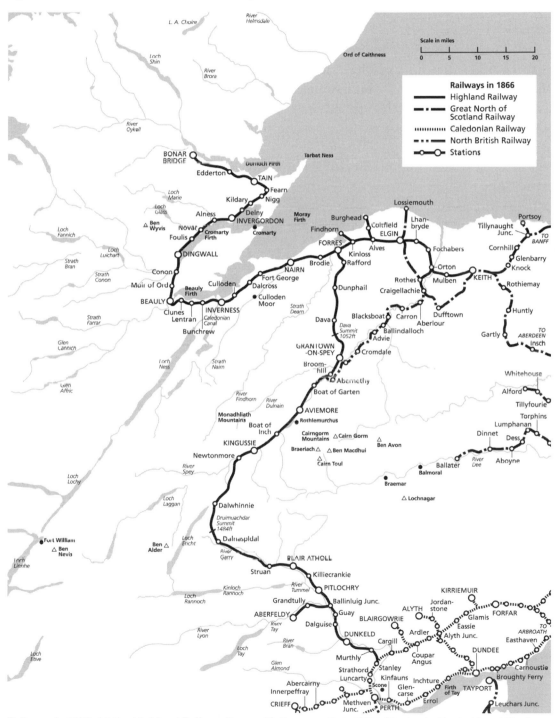

Railways in 1866. All the Highland Railway lines, with the exception of the Stanley to Dunkeld and Findhorn lines had been engineered by Joseph Mitchell, with the assistance of William and Murdoch Paterson.

was involved, with Murdoch, in the survey of the Highland Railway's line from Keith to Portessie, which was approved by Parliament a few days before his death on 29 May 1881. Ironically Joseph Mitchell outlived William Paterson, as he did not die until 26 November 1883.

Murdoch Paterson

After Joseph Mitchell retired in 1867, and with his brother now concentrating on his road work, Murdoch Paterson was in sole charge of the construction of the remainder of Highland Railway lines. He continued the work that he had been carrying out while a partner in Joseph Mitchell and Company, notably the Dingwall and Skye Railway, which it was decided to terminate at Strome Ferry rather than at Kyle of Lochalsh. This was opened on 19 August 1870.

The other scheme that Joseph Mitchell and Company had been involved with was the Sutherland Railway to Golspie. Problems arose here because of the role of William Murray of Geanies, who was a director of the Sutherland and Highland Railways and more importantly a trusted advisor of the 3rd Duke of Sutherland, who was providing much of the finance for the company. Joseph Mitchell resented Murray's interference and submitted the company's resignation as engineers to the Sutherland Railway in 1867. The remaining construction of the line was completed under Kenneth Murray's direction.

The Duke of Sutherland replaced Joseph Mitchell and Company by William Baxter as the engineers to the Sutherland Railway. William Baxter was the engineer for the Duke of Sutherland's Railway from Golspie to Helmsdale, a privately owned line, but presumably used the Mitchell Company's survey as far as Brora. When the Sutherland and Caithness Railway formed to complete the railway to Wick and Thurso, it was decided that William Baxter would be the engineer for the line to the county boundary of Sutherland, but that Murdoch Paterson would be responsible for engineering the line within Caithness to Wick and Thurso. He was also the official engineer for the Sutherland and Caithness. Murdoch seems to have got on far better with the Duke of Sutherland than the rather prickly Joseph Mitchell.

The final link from Helmsdale to Wick and Thurso was opened on 28 July 1874. At the time this was completed Murdoch Paterson was still acting in a consulting capacity to the Highland Railway and its associated companies. In 1865 John Buttle, previously the permanent way superintendent of the Scottish North Eastern Railway, had been appointed superintendent of ways and works; the post was later redesignated resident engineer. In 1868 it was found that he had used HR staff in building a house for himself and he resigned. The HR subsequently bought the house, Carlton Villa, for use by its locomotive superintendent (see page 55).

John Buttle's successor was Peter Wilson of Glasgow, who was appointed resident engineer. He seems to have carried out his duties well enough. On 6 November 1874, however, the HR board was informed that Wilson was ill and, it appears, not expected to return to work in the near future. It was decided that the civil engineer's department would be put under the charge of Murdoch Paterson, 'whose great experience and intimate knowledge of all the works over the whole of the Company's system qualify him in a peculiar manner for the appointment.' On 1 June 1875 the appointment was made permanent.

After the line to Wick was opened on 28 July 1874 Murdoch's railway consultancy work declined and this was probably a major reason why he moved to be an employee of the Highland. He was allowed by the Board to continue work on the Inverness Gas & Water Company's scheme (for supplying water to the town from Loch Ashie) until the Bill for it received parliamentary approval. Another of his major civil engineering projects, the Bridge of Wick, was already under construction.

When Murdoch Paterson became the engineer-in-chief of the Highland Railway he was responsible for the permanent way, structures and signalling of all the lines of the company and its subsidiaries. He also had to deal with the results of snow blockages, a duty which he shared with his assistant William Smith, whose diary forms the basis of the next chapter. John Edgar Campbell recalled in *The Iron Track Through the Highlands* that:

> *It was perhaps at the snowblocks – and there were SOME snowblocks in those days – that Mr Paterson was at his best. He was a born general, and knew how to take the most out of men without assuming the role of a slave driver. He, on such occasions, made himself one of themselves and his directions were usually in such language as 'we'll do this boys or we'll do that…'.*

Murdoch Paterson (1826–1898). Murdoch was described as 'the most genial and kindly of men – a man, it might almost be said, idolised by those under his charge'. He was said to know almost every worker on the line, greeting them with 'Well, how are you getting on *boddach*?'. Murdoch's elder son, also Donald, had worked on the HR as an assistant civil engineer, but had died before his father in 1885. A nephew, also Donald, was an engineer in Singapore.

The extract continued by stating that whatever Murdoch wanted his 'Shovel Brigade' to do, they would carry out. Although he was an abstemious man himself he would ensure that there was 'a sufficient, if not copious supply' of whisky available in the van of the 'Snowblock Special' to refresh his men.

In the 1880s and 1890s Murdoch was responsible for planning a number of branch lines: the one to Portessie opened in 1884, Strathpeffer in 1885, Hopeman in 1892,

Fochabers in 1893, Fortrose in 1894 and Fort George in 1899. At the same time Murdoch was involved in preparing two major extensions to the HR. One was the 34½-mile Aviemore direct line, which shortened the distance to Inverness from the south. This was authorised in 1884, but only completed in 1898. Its main role was to maintain the HR's monopoly of Inverness traffic as other companies were proposing to build lines to the Highland capital. The second scheme was the 10½-mile extension of the Dingwall & Skye line from Strome Ferry to Kyle of Lochalsh, authorised in 1893 and opened on 2 November 1897.

Fort George station in 1913 with 0–4–4 T 45 on the branch train from Gollanfield Junction. The station was in the village of Ardesier, but it was named after the nearby military barracks, which supplied much of the traffic for the 1½-mile branch opened in 1899. It was the last line engineered by Murdoch Paterson; the construction was carried out under his successor on the HR, William Roberts.

The Aviemore and Kyle lines were major projects for Murdoch Paterson, whose health was beginning to deteriorate by 1890. There was, theoretically, some help available from Sir John Fowler, who was appointed consulting engineer to the HR in 1882, but his significant involvement appears to have been mainly limited to the design concepts of the major bridges on the Aviemore line. As Fowler was also the consulting engineer for several other railway companies and was engineer-in chief of the Forth Bridge, which opened in 1890, he would have had limited time to devote to HR affairs.

In October 1891 the HR board agreed that because of his state of health, Murdoch Paterson needed more practical assistance. William Roberts, surveyor of roads for the Badenoch district, who had previously worked for Murdoch, was appointed assistant engineer with responsibility for the lines already open. Murdoch Paterson thereafter concentrated on the lines under construction, principally the Kyle and Aviemore lines, with the latter increasingly taking up the majority of his time.

Culloden Viaduct under construction in the mid-1890s. Running across the centre is the contractor's railway which supplied stone for the viaduct. Murdoch Paterson was born at Dell of Inshes farm 4½ miles from the viaduct and died in the station house at Culloden Moor while supervising the completion of the construction work. David Reid, who was the HR's resident engineer for this section of line, later became a consulting engineer in Inverness.

Culloden Viaduct, Murdoch Paterson's greatest work. The sandstone bridge has 28 50ft arches and a central arch of 100ft over the river Nairn 130ft below. It was originally intended to build it with stone piers and steel girders, like the Findhorn bridge at Tomatin. After consultation with Sir John Fowler, it was decided to make it a masonry structure and there is little doubt that this decision produced a far more impressive viaduct.

By 1898 the greater part of the Aviemore direct line, including the difficult route through Slochd and the viaduct over the Findhorn at Tomatin, had been completed. One great structure remained to be finished – the viaduct over the Nairn at Culloden, the longest masonry bridge in Scotland. This had been a troublesome project. There were problems in finding secure foundations for some of the viaduct piers and the original contractors went bankrupt in 1894.

The Culloden viaduct was nearing completion in the summer of 1898, but some work remained to be done. Murdoch Paterson, by now a sick man, wished to oversee the completion of his most important engineering work and took up residence in the house that had been built for the stationmaster at Culloden Moor. It was here that he died, at the age of 72, on 9 August 1898. Family tradition tells that a few days earlier, realising his end was approaching, he asked the navvies to push him across Culloden Viaduct on a trolley so he could cross it before his death. The Aviemore line was opened through to Inverness on 1 November 1898.

William Roberts and his sons

William Roberts, who succeeded Murdoch Paterson as engineer-in-chief in 1898, came from a railway family. His father, also William (see page 11), had been the HR's superintendent of the line, but had retired through ill health in 1875. He then became a

Achanor in Crown Drive, which was Murdoch Paterson's final home in Inverness. He had previously lived in houses in Brown Street and Millburn when his first wife was alive. Murdoch lived in Ness Bank and then in Crown Circus with his second wife before moving to Achanor. It was from this house that Murdoch's large funeral procession set out on 13 August 1898. As well as the HR heads of departments and engineering staff, many of Murdoch's workmen followed the coffin to Tomnahurich cemetery.

farmer at Dell of Inshes, the same farm where Murdoch Paterson's father had also once been a tenant. One of William senior's other sons, James Roberts, was in charge of the North British Railway locomotive shed at Dundee. When the Tay Bridge collapsed on 28 December 1879, it was James Roberts who crawled out along the bridge from Dundee and established that the central section had collapsed.

William Roberts (1848–1918). As well as leading a busy life as a civil engineer, William was actively involved in public life. He was the chief magistrate of Kingussie, and then a JP in Inverness and a member of the Inverness Burgh School Board.

William Roberts trained as a surveyor and engineer with Peter MacBey of Elgin and joined Murdoch Paterson's engineering staff in the early 1870s to work on the Caithness & Sutherland Railway. He then gained further civil engineering experience in India before returning to Scotland in the mid-1870s to supervise the construction of the railway from Dunfermline to North Queensferry.

By 1881 William Roberts was back in the Highlands working as a surveyor for roads and bridges in the Badenoch district, where he also had a flourishing civil engineering and surveying practice that included architectural work. In 1891, at Murdoch Paterson's suggestion, he was appointed Murdoch's deputy on the HR. His role was to be engineer for the lines already open, including preparing plans for the doubling of the southern part of the main line. William Roberts accepted the appointment, on the condition that he would become Murdoch's successor as engineer-in-chief of the HR.

As Murdoch Paterson's health declined, the scope of William's work increased and he became involved with the construction of the Kyle extension, the Aviemore Line and the branch line to Fort George. This was in addition to the doubling of the main line to Aviemore. Although powers were obtained in an Act for doubling the section from Stanley Junction to Aviemore in 1897, financial constraints meant that only the section from Blair Atholl to Dalwhinnie over Druimuachdar summit was doubled; this work was completed in 1909. This section was particularly heavily used because of banking locomotives returning south from Dalwhinnie.

Other major work followed in the 15 years that William Roberts was engineer-in-chief. The viaducts over the Spey at Orton and over the River Beauly were replaced by steel structures, as were more than 100 cast-iron bridges. In 1913 the first part of the work of doubling the line to the north between Clachnaharry and Clunes was completed.

The Highland Railway was in a poor financial state in the early 1900s and could not expand further. The only two new lines that William Roberts engineered were the Dornoch and the Wick & Lybster Light Railways. These were built under the Light Railways Act of 1896, which was designed to reduce the costs of construction. Both were built by independent companies who found that the HR was prepared to strike a hard

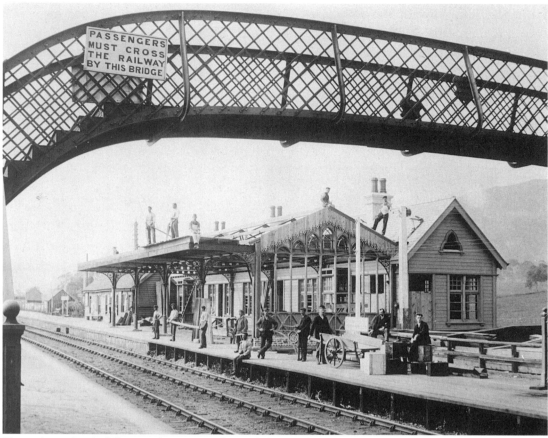

The main station buildings under construction at Aviemore in 1897, in preparation for the station becoming a junction for the two routes to Inverness. The original basic station building of the 1860s can be seen on the left. The awning with glazed ends is similar to that at Kingussie, which was rebuilt in 1894, although the main buildings at Kingussie were of stone. The design of these two stations was carried out under the direction of William Roberts.

The original box girder bridge across the Spey at Orton (see page 28) was replaced by a steel lattice girder bridge in 1906. This photograph shows the steelwork for the new bridge being erected inside the old girders.

The Mound station in 1902, just after the Dornoch Light Railway, curving away to the right, had been completed. The resident engineer for this was Donald Roberts. The signal cabin and signals shown in this photograph were also the responsibility of the civil engineering department.

financial bargain to protect its own interests. After completion the HR worked and maintained the light railways.

William Roberts was the engineer for both of these lines and in each case one of his sons was a resident engineer. Donald Roberts was a resident engineer for the Dornoch line, opened in 1902, and Billy Roberts was a resident engineer for the Lybster line, which opened in 1903. A third son, Ewan, also worked in the engineer's department of the HR.

William Roberts's expertise in the construction of railways in remote places was called upon in 1897 when he and Joseph Tatlow, general manager of the Midland Great Western Railway of Ireland, were asked to report on a proposed light railway in Donegal. This was at the request of Thomas Robertson, chairman of the Irish Board of Works, which would have to help to finance any line. Thomas Robertson had started his working life on the Highland Railway and had succeeded William Roberts senior as superintendent of the line in 1875.

Joseph Tatlow records that he and William Roberts held several public meetings and drove 240 miles by horse and trap to inspect the Londonderry & Lough Swilly's proposed line between Letterkenny and Burtonport. The proposal was approved. He described William as being 'a capable, energetic, practical man, and a canny Scot'. The HR's civil engineering link with Ireland continued the following year when William Roberts's chief assistant engineer, T.M. Batchen, went to work as engineer for the Irish Board of Works, obviously on his chief's recommendation.

Lybster station on the occasion of the inspection of the Wick and Lybster Light Railway by Colonel Druitt of the Board of Trade on 26 June 1903. William Roberts stands second from the left on the platform. Third from the left is William Whitelaw, the HR chairman. Billy Roberts, who along with Thomas Fairlie was resident engineer for the line, stands second from the left in the group at the front of the platform.

The family of William and Madeline Roberts, about 1900. From left to right sitting are Ewan, Billy, Cecil, Isabella Fraser (mother of Madeline and widow of Donald Fraser, stationmaster at Broomhill), William, Ian and Ella. Standing are Lena, Tommy, Madeline, Donald and Hamish. The Roberts household at Rockburn, Southside Road, Inverness, was completed by Jane Munro, the cook and Christina MacLean, the maid.

In October 1913 William Roberts, having reached the age of 65, retired. From 1916, however, he was extremely busy in a new role as food commissioner for the north of Scotland during World War One. In the autumn of 1918 he contracted influenza on a visit to the Western Isles in stormy weather. His health deteriorated after he received news of the death of one of his sons, Hamish, just before the end of the war and he died on 1 December 1918. His obituary noted that all seven of his sons had joined the forces voluntarily during the war.

The Roberts engineering tradition continued with the three sons who had worked on the Highland Railway. After five years on the Highland, Donald successively worked for the North Eastern Railway, the Central Argentine Railway, in Canada and for Sir William Arrol, the civil engineering contractor. Following service with the Royal Engineers he was selected to take charge of building airfields for the Royal Flying Corps in Britain towards the end of World War One. After the war Donald's civil engineering career included working for the London & North Eastern Railway. Billy moved to the Buenos Aires Great Southern Railway in the 1900s and, after service in World War One, became the county surveyor of Sutherland. Ian, who like his brothers had served in the Royal Engineers, became a mechanical and electrical engineer at the LMS works in Crewe before moving to the Iraq State Railways.

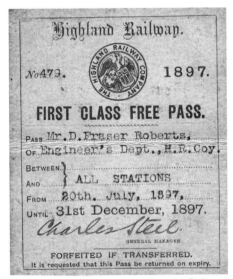

First-class pass issued to Donald Roberts when he was working in the civil engineer's department of the Highland Railway.

Willie Paterson

One of William Roberts's last acts as engineer-in-chief of the Highland Railway in 1913 was to appoint Willie Paterson, the great-nephew of his predecessor Murdoch Paterson, to the post of apprentice engineer. This must have given William Roberts much satisfaction as he was a great admirer of his former chief.

The new HR engineer-in-chief was Alexander Newlands, who had originally come from Elgin. Like William Roberts he had been apprenticed to the Elgin firm of Gordon and MacBey, surveyors and engineers. He joined the HR in 1892 and worked as resident engineer on the Kyle of Lochalsh extension and then the doubling of the line from Blair Atholl to Dalwhinnie. In 1898 he was appointed chief assistant engineer and then in 1902 he became William Roberts's deputy.

Alexander Newlands appointed Archie McMurdo as his chief assistant engineer. He had started his railway civil engineering career on the Glasgow & South Western Railway in 1901 and came to the HR as a general assistant in 1910.

In 1913 the major work in hand on the HR was the completion of the doubling of the line to Clunes. Another light railway, from Conon to Cromarty, was under construction.

The engineers for this were Formans and McCall, who had been responsible for the West Highland Railway, but as the Highland Railway was to work the line, the HR civil engineers maintained a general oversight of the work. This line was never completed.

It may not have appeared that there was a particularly demanding programme of work for the civil engineering department on the Highland in 1914, but events were to prove otherwise. On 18 June 1914 a cloudburst swept away the Baddengorm Burn bridge north of Carr Bridge just as the 10.00am train from Glasgow to Inverness was crossing, with the loss of five lives. Alexander Newlands organised the completion of the new bridge by the contractor, Sir Robert McAlpine, in three weeks.

Rebuilding work taking place at the site of the Baddengorm Burn railway bridge on 30 June 1914, only 12 days after the original bridge had been swept away by floodwater. The workmen of Sir Robert McAlpine have already made good progress on the construction work.

An event of far greater consequence was the outbreak of World War One in August 1914. The Highland Railway provided the main supply line to the British Grand Fleet base at Scapa Flow as well as the vastly expanded naval depot at Invergordon. It also had to carry coal and other traffic that had previously come north by coastal shipping, which was now withdrawn. There were vast numbers of additional trains and there were occasions in wartime when every siding between Perth and Wick was full of wagons.

The Highland civil engineers had to react by laying new sidings. The diary of an HR junior civil engineer, name unknown, which survives in the Highland Council Archives, records that Willie Paterson was involved in surveying for additional sidings at Invergordon in 1916. In March 1917 Willie was surveying at Orbliston in connection

Rose Street signal cabin, Inverness, being moved in March 1918. The signalman had difficulty in seeing over Rose Street Bridge in its previous location, so the building, complete with its locking frame, was jacked up and moved 110 yards on bogies. It was then turned at right angles into its final position shown here. A year earlier Willie Paterson and his colleagues had surveyed the area to finalise the cabin's new site.

with 'a wood carting system'. Many trees were being felled in the area to replace timber which before the war had come from Scandinavia for uses such as pit props.

Willie Paterson was also involved in one of the strangest incidents on the HR during World War One, when the new River class 4–6–0s were rejected by Alexander Newlands on the grounds that they were too heavy for the line. O.S. Nock, the railway author, described how Willie Paterson had told him that he and everyone else in the civil engineer's department was asked to check the stress the engines would cause on major bridges. There

The viaduct across the Findhorn near Forres. This photograph was taken by J.A. Dale of the HR civil engineer's department. The diary of a junior engineer, which survives in the Highland Archives, records how in 1916 Dale had organised the protection of one of the abutments with large stones, to prevent it being undermined due to a change in the course of the river.

has been much controversy about the rejection of these locomotives, but the HR civil engineers were certainly concerned about the state of the railway's bridges, which were carrying vast amounts of extra wartime traffic. The junior engineer's diary shows that much time was spent by staff, including Willie Paterson, on examining bridges in 1916–17. The 1858 bridge over the Findhorn near Forres on the line to Keith received particular attention, with surveys also being taken of the riverbed.

After the end of the war Alexander Newlands was awarded the CBE and Archie McMurdo the MBE for their wartime work. Peace brought some respite for the civil engineer's section. The staff still, however, had to deal with the extremes of weather. On 8 July 1923, seven months after the London Midland & Scottish Railway had been formed, there was another major washout north of Carr Bridge. The railway bridges crossing the Bogbain burn and the Carr Bridge–Inverness road were swept away, as well as a girder bridge near Slochd. Sir Robert McAlpine was again the firm that carried out the rebuilding of the bridges under Alexander Newlands's direction, as for the Baddengorm bridge rebuilding in 1913. Willie Paterson was away from home for several weeks while he supervised the rebuilding work on site. The railway reopened on 31 August.

A group of Highland Railway civil engineering staff in the office in Inverness in 1922. The figure on the left is believed to be Archie McMurdo (1880–1959) who was then the chief assistant engineer; in LMS days he became the Inverness district engineer and later the Scottish divisional engineer. The identities of the others are not known, but may include Skene Sclanders, who came from Nairn. Most of those who joined the HR civil engineer's department as apprentice engineers came from the area around Inverness.

The formation of the LMS was to open up wider opportunities for the HR civil engineers. In 1925 Alexander Newlands was appointed divisional engineer for the former London & North Western Railway system based at Crewe and in 1927 he became the chief civil engineer for the London Midland & Scottish Railway, which was the most important railway civil engineering post in the country. Alexander Newlands retired in 1933 and died in 1938. In his retirement in Glasgow he was a director of Hurst Nelson, the Motherwell carriage and wagon builders.

When Alexander Newlands was transferred south in 1925 Archie McMurdo moved up to become the district engineer in Inverness. Willie Paterson, who had been an engineering assistant since 1919, became the chief assistant. In 1929 Archie McMurdo was promoted again to be the permanent way assistant to Alexander Newlands at the LMS civil engineering headquarters in London. Willie Paterson was promoted to be the Inverness district engineer, only 16 years after beginning his railway career. A few years later Archie McMurdo returned to Scotland as the divisional engineer for the LMS.

In the 1930s there was emphasis on cutting costs and introducing more efficient working on the railways. When Willie Paterson was in charge at Inverness a system of motorised trolleys was introduced. This meant that gangs of permanent way staff could cover longer sections on the Wick and Kyle lines. Other changes included the lifting of most of the branch line to Portessie in 1937.

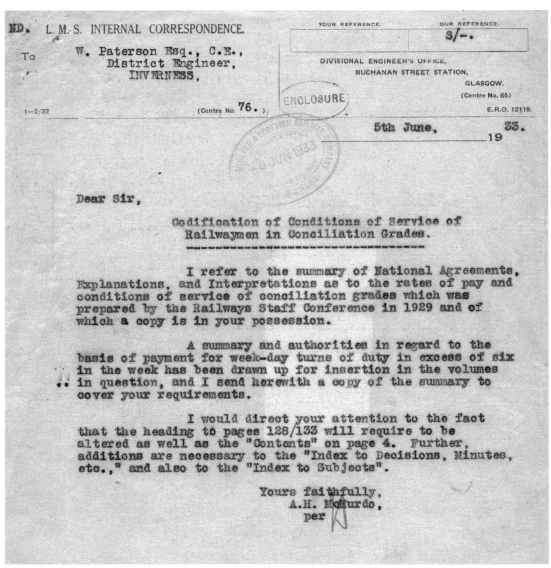

Letter about staff conditions of service from A.H. McMurdo, the LMS Scottish Divisional Engineer, to his former HR colleague, Willie Paterson, the Inverness district engineer.

Any further retrenchment on the Highland section of the LMS ceased in 1939 with the outbreak of World War Two. Just as a quarter of a century earlier, Willie found himself involved in projects to increase the capacity of the line to cope with the wartime traffic. He soon had to deal with a difficult war situation in a completely different environment when in 1940 he was appointed civil engineer on the Glasgow central district, one of the largest on the LMS. The link with the Highland Railway engineers was broken with Willie Paterson's departure from Inverness, as his successor was Ian Frazer, the LMS assistant engineer at Derby South who had started his career on the Caledonian Railway in 1914. Ian Frazer later became the chief civil engineer for the Scottish Region of British Railways.

In 1954 Willie Paterson was appointed to be the assistant engineer responsible for the engineering work for British Railways' Glasgow suburban electrification, which included rebuilding bridges, lowering track and building new stations. He retired in 1961 just after the first electric 'blue trains' had been introduced.

Willie Paterson was closely involved with his professional organisations. He was vice-president of the Permanent Way Institute for 15 years and was chairman of the Glasgow and West of Scotland Association of the Institute of Civil Engineers. He was one of the Institution's examiners for many years.

Working for Willie Paterson clearly provided good training. Two of the engineers who were his pupils when studying for their engineering qualifications subsequently went on to senior railway positions. Bill McMurdo (the son of his former colleague) became the chief civil engineer for the Eastern Region and Archie Paterson (no relation) became the Chief Civil Engineer of the British Railways Board.

There is little doubt that Willie inherited his great-uncle Murdoch Paterson's geniality. The *Inverness Courier* wrote after his death in July 1964 of 'his good humour and kindly interest in others'. It also recorded that he had been a leading figure in the Highland sport of shinty for almost 50 years. He was the president of the Camanachd Association, the sport's ruling body, from 1937 to 1948. In the early 1950s there was still a member of the Kingussie permanent way squad who was allowed to leave early on Saturday mornings to prepare to play for the town's shinty team!

Willie Paterson (1896–1964). Willie Paterson was a native of Beauly and lived there during the time he worked at the civil engineer's office in Inverness. He was involved with several local organisations and when he left for Glasgow in 1940 the *Inverness Courier* wrote that 'his departure from Beauly will leave a blank in the social life of the village.' Willie Paterson returned to Beauly after his retirement in 1961.

CHAPTER 3

A Year in the Life of a Civil Engineer
William Smith

In the Highland Council Archives are documents which give brief, but fascinating, glimpses into the lives and work of two of Murdoch Paterson's assistants in the 1880s and 1890s: William Smith and Murdoch MacDonald. William Smith's diary runs from February 1880 to July 1881, with details added of a few significant projects in later years. This chapter concentrates on the diary entries from May 1880 to May 1881, with additional information drawn from contemporary issues of the *Inverness Courier* and the minute books of the Highland Railway directors. It also looks briefly at some of his later projects.

William Smith was described by John Edgar Campbell in *The Iron Track Through the Highlands* as Murdoch Paterson's 'valued assistant', who rose from the ranks and was 'like his chief a favourite with everyone because of his geniality'. It must be said that some of his comments about his colleagues in the diary were not always generous, but this was his own private record of what was a sometimes demanding job.

The blower on the Burghead branch, which deflected sand away from the line and prevented blockages, was based on an idea of William Smith's. He recorded that the sand was 'a torment' and it had cost £80 to clear away one blockage. Similar blowers were installed, on both sides of the line, to prevent snow blockages in Caithness. The identity of the figure pointing out the blower is not known, but it seems possible it could be William Smith, especially as it was probably taken in 1900 by R.A. Dale, who was also a member of the HR civil engineering staff.

Part of William Smith's work was in the civil engineer's office at Inverness. Some of this was routine, such as dealing with correspondence. He also spent time preparing plans for buildings. Another task he recorded was colouring plans in connection with the Bill for the amalgamation of the Dingwall and Skye with the Highland Railway, which came before Parliament in July 1880.

Invershin, the first station in Sutherland, in the 1950s. The goods store, which William Smith surveyed the site of in May 1880, is at the far end of the platform.

William Smith was often out on site on the line; this involved much travelling from Inverness. On 27 and 28 May 1880 he was in Sutherland in connection with a drain at Helmsdale, a ditch at Golspie, a water pipe at Rogart and also finalising the site for the goods shed at Invershin. In December he was similarly involved with the site of a shed and crane at Kinloss. Other work during the year included surveying a siding at Dingwall and additional land at Fowlis. Inspecting bridges was another duty and he records examining and planning further work on the bridges at Beauly, Attadale and over the Spey at Orton.

Accidents

In 1880–1 William Smith often took charge of dealing with the aftermath of accidents and of the fierce snowstorms which swept the Highlands that winter. On one occasion he had to deal with the aftermath of both at the same time.

On 15 July 1880 William travelled to Newtonmore, where a locomotive and tender had been derailed at the turntable. They were rerailed and the track repaired in a fairly short time. On 17 August a pilot engine was derailed on the south points at Dalwhinnie. Six days later there was a more serious incident at Tain when 11 wagons were derailed

The bridge over the River Beauly with one of the original wooden sections on the left and the new steel section constructed by Head Wrightson in 1881 on the right. William Smith visited the bridge on a number of occasions in 1880–1, probably because of concern about the state of the structure that was about to be replaced. On 4 February 1881 he recorded that there was a solid foot of ice under the bridge. This photograph was taken in 1909 when both the wooden approaches and the 1881 bridge were about to be replaced (see page 71).

at the north points and damaged the permanent way. William Smith arrived at 12 noon by the 9.40am from Inverness and carried out some rerailing and repairs to the track, but it was 8pm before the travelling crane arrived from Inverness and all the wagons could be moved. William only arrived home at 10.40am the next day.

The next accident that William attended was one that had consequences for the operation of the Highland Railway system. On 16 October there was a collision, or a 'pitchup' in William's words, at Ballinluig. A southbound goods train hit a northbound mixed passenger and goods train which had stopped foul of the crossover. By the time he arrived there the line was clear and he returned home. Three days later he returned to Ballinluig by the night train to meet Major-General Hutchinson, the Board of Trade inspector, who was conducting an investigation into the accident. It was a very frosty night and, in addition to the greatcoat he was wearing, Mr Critchley, the Inverness stationmaster, supplied him with a further greatcoat and a pillow to make his journey more comfortable.

On arrival at Ballinluig at 6am the next day William measured the distances between the signals and the points before meeting Hutchinson, and waited until the latter had completed his investigation. As a result of the inspector's investigations there were changes to signals at certain stations.

Snowstorms and hurricanes

William Smith notes other derailments in his diary, but his entries for the four months from November 1880 are dominated by dealing with the consequences of severe weather, which the *Inverness Courier* described as worse than any winter since 1838. The first snow fell in October with William recording three inches between Dalwhinnie and Dava on the 20th of that month.

Small snowploughs at Inverness shed. They were fitted to engines as soon as snow was expected.

During the night of 16–17 November a great snowstorm blew up over the Highlands. William rose at 3am and went out at 6.30am. The telegraph wires were broken at the Divie viaduct and this was a serious problem as the line was worked by block telegraph and train order. Locomotives with snowploughs managed to clear the line and William travelled to both Keith and Grantown before returning home at 3pm. Snow continued to fall during the next few days, but the snowploughs kept the line open.

Snow continued to fall in December and on 18 December there was a southwesterly gale. William travelled as far as Kincraig, recording that one train had become stuck at Dalwhinnie. A thaw had set in by 21 December, but this was only temporary and it snowed heavily on Christmas Day.

The *Inverness Courier* recorded on 27 December that there had been no trains north of Helmsdale for three days, but that squads of surfacemen were beginning to clear the line. Further snowstorms hampered their efforts and the HR in Caithness was blocked until 31 December.

On 31 December 1880 William Smith set out for Helmsdale, 'paying the men along the line'. On arrival at Helmsdale he went to a hotel and stayed until 1.30am on New Year's morning. He then went to the waiting room at the station, where he joined other

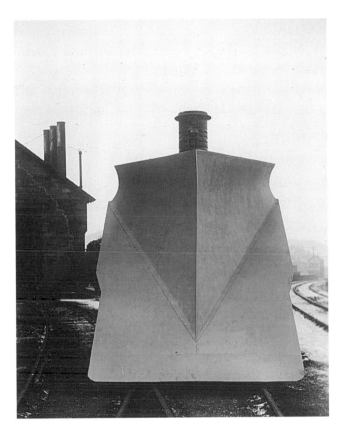

One of the Highland Railway's large snowploughs, fitted to a Jones Goods 4–6–0 and photographed at Inverness in the 1890s. The first of this type of snowplough was designed by William Stroudley, the HR's locomotive superintendent, in 1866. These large ploughs were in constant use during the 1880–1 winter.

passengers who were waiting for the train that should have left at 3.30pm the previous day. They passed the time by singing and reciting before the train left, probably about nine hours late. William had breakfast when he got home and then went to bed before rising and going into Inverness in the afternoon of New Year's Day. Here he saw 'Scenes of drunkenness and foolish pleasure and certainly a fearful example before a family…', a reminder that over-indulgence in alcohol is not a modern phenomenon.

On 14 January 1881 the weather caused a further problem for the Highland Railway. The heating apparatus was lit for the Inverness shed water tank, which had presumably frozen, at 9am. At 11am one of the bottom plates of the tank burst with a large bang. The force of the water knocked out a door and window underneath the tank, fractured a water column and cascaded water all over the adjoining ground.

Clearing snow from the line on the Highland Railway. Dealing with the aftermath of the snowstorms occupied William Smith for a significant part of the winter of 1880–1.

On 20 January what both William and the local press described as a 'hurricane' raged throughout the Highlands, with snow drifting from the north-east. On this 'fearful morning' William Smith was called out at 8am. At 10.20am he left Inverness with a special train, conveying 150 men to free the 5.40am to Forres which had become stuck in snow at Castle Stuart, just over a mile west of Dalcross station. The special then proceeded eastwards, but became stuck in a cutting east of Nairn.

William was supervising the clearance of the cutting when, to his alarm, the 9.30am from Perth was seen 'tearing along at a fearful speed throwing snow in all directions', toward the men working with spades and picks in the cutting. He just had time to get the men clear, but the two locomotives of the 9.30am struck the first locomotive of the works train, which had been stuck, with considerable force. This engine had been uncoupled from the remainder of the train, but it was pushed back to hit the second engine, which then sent the van and carriage used by workmen back another 300 yards. The cylinders of these two engines were broken and the *Inverness Courier* recorded that the snowploughs were 'smashed to pieces'. A driver and a fireman were cut in the face, but the 40 passengers on the train from Perth escaped with a severe shaking. Several, however, later claimed compensation from the HR.

William writes in his diary, in an understated way, that they 'got all clear at last' and started for home at 7am on Friday morning. He must have arrived back at his house 24 hours after first being called out. On 24 January he went to Nairn to pay some of the staff who had come out to clear the snow on the Thursday evening and recorded that they had no complaints about the pay of three shillings. The following day William

Three HR locos charging a snowdrift. When William Smith was supervising the clearance of a cutting near Nairn on 20 January 1881 he saw, to his horror, a train coming straight towards the workmen: 'tearing along throwing snow in all directions'.

Smith returned to Nairn to pay the remainder of the men and also took measurements at the scene of the collision where a government inspector had arrived to carry out his investigation into the accident.

It was hardly surprising that the half yearly report of the Highland Railway, which covered the period to 28 February 1881, recorded that traffic had suffered from the long and severe winter in the north of Scotland and that working expenses had increased.

The snow and ice continued throughout the winter and into the spring. The Perth line was blocked again at Dava in early March and a considerable length of telegraph wire brought down. The continued severity of the weather is shown by the fact that the Caledonian Canal was cleared of ice in early April. Even more remarkably William Smith wrote of very stormy showers of snow when he walked between Forsinard and Altnabreac on 6 May 1881.

Later work

At the end of William's diary are notes on specific projects. They are undated, but seem to be from the early and mid-1880s. They include the viaduct over the Findhorn at Forres, the Mulben burn and the site of the new station at Dingwall which was erected in 1885.

Another project in the mid-1880s was the design of a new carriage shed at Needlefield to replace the shed being sold to MacDonald Fraser for incorporation in their new auction market building. William Smith designed the framework to use old rails rather than cast-iron pillars. It was suggested that he should take out a patent for this, but he declined.

Dingwall station in 1913 showing the 1885 station building, with its elaborate platform canopy, under the footbridge. To its left is the original station building of 1862. The first plan had been to build the new structure on the site of the old, but William Smith successfully argued against this.

Similarly William did not take out a patent for his proposal for a blower fence to keep the railway on the Burghead branch clear of sand after Murdoch Paterson had vetoed the erection of the blower. He instead encouraged a Mr Howie to take up the idea and apply to the HR for a trial, which proved very successful.

Railway, natural history and family diary entries

William Smith's diary does not only relate to his work. He also notes events which happened around his home at Oriflamme cottage at Millburn on the outskirts of Inverness, close to the railway to Forres. Some of the entries refer to the railway, while others relate to his natural history interests and his family.

The railway entries include one for 24 June 1880 when sparks from a special fish train set fire to a nearby plantation and destroyed a great part of it. William recorded that the fire looked very alarming '…and seemed to defy all our exertions to get it put out.' A happier observation was the locomotive department's excursion to Perth passing on 2 July with the engine 'gaily decorated'. The freemasons' excursion on 31 July ran in two portions. The first, of seven vehicles, had flags flying and pipes playing, while the second, of five vehicles, had a band playing.

On 1 and 2 November William noted that the locomotive belonging to the contractor building the Cameron Barracks was being moved along the roadway. On 25 November a sheep van was blown down the line from the goods sidings and a locomotive had to be sent out to collect it.

0–4–2 T *Needlefield*, which was the carriage works shunter at Inverness in 1880. On 1 November William Smith recorded this engine hauling a locomotive belonging to John Coghill, the contractor for the Cameron Barracks building, out to the level crossing gates at Millburn. The HR had agreed to provide a temporary siding, at Coghill's expense, so that the contractor could bring in building material. This had obviously not been completed by November 1880, as William records it being taken off the rails and moved along Millburn Road.

An interest in natural history and geology comes through in the diary. William had a small menagerie of wild animals at the back of his house. He also had a collection of 'relics and curios', which included fossils he had collected when out on the line. William was a member of the Inverness Field Club.

William Smith died at his home on 15 September 1909 aged 79. His obituary in the *Inverness Courier* stated that he was 'for years a valued assistant to the late Murdoch Paterson' and he had retired from active work a number of years before. He had been involved in many improvements carried out on the HR and was 'held in high esteem by his fellow employees'.

The Smith family's involvement with the Highland Railway continued through William's younger son, James. There are several references in his father's diary to James, who was five to six years old at that time. In one 'an engine' is bought for him out of part of the proceeds from the sale of honey from the beehives that William kept. James is later recorded as having a run with his engine and squirrel; presumably both were wooden toys with wheels.

The toy engine proved an appropriate present for James, as he became an apprentice fitter at Lochgorm Works in 1891 at the age of 16 and then worked in the drawing office before progressing to locomotive inspector. In 1898 he became the first shed foreman at Aviemore (page 112), moving to Inverness in 1916. Here he had to cope with the massive demands for motive power during the last years of World War One.

After the formation of the LMS James Smith was appointed the chief district locomotive superintendent for Inverness, covering the area from Aviemore to Wick and Kyle of Lochalsh to Keith. He retired in 1935 and died in 1940. Engineering clearly ran in the blood of the Smiths because the obituary for James mentions that his elder son was a mining engineer in Vancouver.

Looking east towards Welsh's Bridge, which led to Millburn House, on the outskirts of Inverness. Just visible through the bridge is the ticket platform and Carlton Villa, which was the locomotive superintendent's house. On the right of the railway is Millburn Road, which William Smith walked along from his home to the civil engineer's office. He mentions taking his young son, James, for walks up to the bridge.

CHAPTER 4

A Notable Apprentice Engineer in the 1890s
Murdoch MacDonald

In his book *Iron Track Through the Highlands* John Edgar Campbell described Murdoch MacDonald as 'A Notable Apprentice' (of Murdoch Paterson).

A collection of letters and other papers relating to Murdoch MacDonald survives in the Highland Council Archives. The documents, covering several aspects of his life between 1889 and 1895, show that Murdoch appears to have been a charismatic person, a keen sportsman, and someone who was able to carry out five private civil engineering commissions at the same time as energetically working for the Highland Railway.

Murdoch MacDonald was born in Inverness in 1866 and entered the HR service as a civil engineering apprentice in 1884. From 1890 to 1894 he was the resident engineer responsible for the construction of the 13½-mile Black Isle branch from Muir of Ord to Fortrose; the authorised final two-mile section to Rosemarkie was never built. The *North Star* newspaper reported that at the banquet for the opening of the Black Isle line in February 1894 Murdoch Paterson had said that 'Mr MacDonald had not only borne the heat and burden of the day in summer, but the cold storms of winter as well, and his ability and energy promised a happy and prosperous future.'

Murdoch MacDonald from an illustration in the *North Star* for 15 February 1894 which reported on the opening of the Black Isle Railway. The report said he was one of Murdoch Paterson's 'disciples and greatest admirers. In fact to see him at work one can at once perceive that he, in great measure, possesses Mr Paterson's professional "go".'

The *North Star* then mentioned that Murdoch's abilities had also been appreciated by a Black Isle landowner, J.D. Fletcher (who was about to become an influential HR director). Fletcher, who had inherited and expanded a fortune made abroad, was carrying out extensive improvements to his estate of Rosehaugh. These included the extension of his mansion to become one of the largest in the Highlands and the construction of new buildings and embankments, as well as the building of a hydro-electric scheme to provide light for his houses. Whereas the architectural work was

Receipted bill from the Tarradale Inn, Muir of Ord, showing charges for a carriage with a driver from the landing where the Kessock ferry from Inverness arrived to Fortrose. This receipt, from among Murdoch MacDonald's surviving papers, is presumably for a journey Murdoch made in connection with drawing up of contract documents for the construction of the Black Isle Railway.

carried out by William Flockhart, a well-known London architect, the civil engineering work was entrusted to the young Murdoch Macdonald.

John Henderson, J.D. Fletcher's factor at Rosehaugh, was also town clerk at Fortrose (for no less than 71 years!), so it is not surprising that Murdoch was also asked to be the engineer for the drainage works in Fortrose. This was in spite of problems with the

Redcastle station in 1907. This was one of the five stations on the Black Isle branch for which Murdoch MacDonald was the resident engineer. The line served the farming and fishing communities of the peninsula on the north of the Moray Firth. On the left is John Mackintosh, porter, and on the right, James Morrison, stationmaster, who later moved to Avoch, further west on the branch, and then to Conon (see page 9).

The Highland Railway Company

Engineer's Office

~~Inverness~~ 28th August 1894
Drumnadrochit,

R. G. Gillanders Esqre
        District Comtee Clerk.
              Rosemarkie,

Dear Sir,

        Avoch Drainage

        I now send you Mr John Ross
the Inspector on above works
note of his time which extends
to 12 weeks. The rate fixed
for him was 30/- per week &
The money thus payable to him
will be £18. (eighteen pounds slg)
which I hereby certify as correct
                Yours faithfully
                Murdoch MacDonald

Letter to the Black Isle District Committee clerk about the Avoch drainage project. Murdoch would have been staying in Drumnadrochit while surveying the HR's proposed line to Fort William.

drains, which Henderson felt were the HR's fault: 'Confound you Railway people. You are the most shuffling quibblers I ever did come across' and 'the most despicable jugglers under the sun' are two of the phrases used by the town clerk in writing to Murdoch MacDonald in January 1895. Nevertheless, Henderson did not bear Murdoch any personal grudges, as he was asking him at the same time for £25 for an investment for a syndicate they were both members of.

Probably because of his involvement in the Fortrose drainage scheme, Murdoch MacDonald then became engineer for the Avoch water supply and drainage schemes and the Munlochy drainage scheme, which he carried out for the Black Isle District Board. He was also involved in planning a hydro-electric scheme for the estate owner at Farr in Inverness-shire. The suppliers of equipment for the latter sent him details of a steel windmill for generating electricity. Murdoch was far ahead of his time in looking at methods of renewable energy.

In addition to his railway and outside civil engineering work, Murdoch MacDonald also managed to find time to pursue his sporting interests. He had been captain and then secretary of Inverness Rovers Football Club in the late 1880s and served as secretary of the North of Scotland Football Association in the early 1890s. He was also one of the Association's 'umpires', or referees, at their cup-ties.

'A Novel Excursion'

During the period he was working as resident engineer on the Black Isle Railway, Murdoch MacDonald struck up a good relationship with the contractor, John Ross of Fearn. Murdoch seems to have worked with him on non-railway civil engineering jobs.

Murdoch took part in a trip from Inverness organised by John Ross to see the work taking place on the Findhorn viaduct at Tomatin. This was one of two sections of the Aviemore to Inverness line for which John Ross was the contractor. The *Scottish Highlander* of 5 July 1894 gave an account of the previous day's trip, headed 'A Novel Excursion', which is worthy of Jerome K. Jerome:

The orthodox carriage and horses were dispensed with on this occasion, and the means of locomotion was by a large and powerful traction engine to which were coupled two large waggons and a brake, the latter supplied by Mr Dick (of Messrs Macrae and Dick). At 9.15am in the morning, the time the excursion started, a large part of townspeople and others, numbering over fifty, had got comfortably seated in the waggons and the journey started with a loud whistle from the engine, a whistling apparatus being specially fitted for the occasion. On leaving the town three hearty cheers were raised. Pipe-Major Ferguson and Piper Fraser, both in full uniform, accompanied the party and the stirring strain of the brace of pipes wielded by the sturdy pipers did much to increase the enjoyment of everyone present. The train, for such it was in reality, kept a uniform pace of four miles an hour. Refreshments were served to the excursionists when a little over four miles had been covered, and it is

Telegraphic Address: TURBINATUS, LONDON.   A.B.C. CODE USED.   TELEPHONIC NUMBER 1903.

FREDERIC NELL.

THE "VICTOR" TURBINE,
SMITH & VAILE PUMPS,
GOULD'S TRIPLEX PUMPS,
PELTON WHEELS,
&c. &c. &c.

SHOW ROOMS & STORES on ground floor.

97, Queen Victoria Street,
London
E.C.   2nd July   189 5.

Murdock MacDonald, Esq.

    Bayfield,

        Midmills Road,

            Inverness.

Dear Sir:-

          Farr Water Supply.

    With reference to our conversation respecting this matter
I understand that water supply is 2 cubic feet per second = 120 cubic
feet per minute and that there are two storage ponds, one 100 feet x
100 feet x 4 ft. deep from which a fall of 27 ft. could be obtained in
a distance of 800 ft. and the second a loch having an area of 35 acres
from which a fall of 23 ft. could be obtained in a distance of 1180 ft.

    I think the best plan would be to use the water from the loch
which would pass through 16" dia. pipes to the turbine and I will
therefore base my calculations upon this source and upon a turbine to
give a maximum power of 9 H.P.

    To develop this power would require 385 cubic feet of water
per minute which in passing through 1180 ft. of 16" pipes would give
a loss of head due to friction equal to 8 ft. reducing the working fall
to 15 ft.

    Under these conditions I would advise a 10 inch turbine

Letter from the firm of Frederick Nell about supplying a turbine to generate electricity at Farr Mills. This is not the only letter from England to misspell Murdoch's Christian name! Other Highland Railway engineers, including William Roberts and Alexander Newlands, had an interest in hydro-electricity.

needless to say that ample justice was given to the various beverages. After a while the excursionists settled down to enjoy themselves, gathering in small groups, one playing nap at a penny a game, another story-telling, and another admiring the beautiful scenery. In this way the journey though long was pleasantly passed over, one or two little 'incidents' only helping to give a spice of romance to the outing. For instance, shortly after leaving the town, the pony which was sent ahead to clear the way bolted up a side road, the rider completely losing control of the animal for a few minutes; and then again further on a rather spirited cart horse shied and rushing up against a milestone slightly damaged the cart and generally frightened the onlookers... By the time Tomatin was reached the 'old stagers' of the party, or rather we should say the businessmen, had completely thrown away the careworn bank-balance look with which they started the journey, and their facial anatomy had assumed quite a boyish and frolicsome smile. As evidence of this, it may be stated that whenever anybody passed the road, hats were doffed and handkerchiefs waved and the air rang with loud hurras.

The visitors having inspected the huge viaduct and admiringly watched the various steam appliances at work... prepared themselves for the principal item of the day – the luncheon. Before going on to the luncheon, it may be of interest to attempt to describe the picture here presented to the spectator. The peaceful river, out of which the massive pillars which form the masonry seem to grow, the many and various puffing and snorting steam engines, the

hundreds of navvies, and the beautiful green herbage of this Highland glen present a picture which will remain in the mind's eye of the fortunate spectator for a lifetime. But the luncheon. It is needless to say that repast, which was served up on the banks of the Findhorn in the inimitable style characteristic of Mr Cesari of the Station Hotel, was literally cleared off the boards by the hungry travellers.

There were then several toasts proposed 'in true Highland fashion' including one to 'the navvies'. John Ross, in his reply to this, said that 'the

The Findhorn viaduct to the south of Tomatin on the direct line from Aviemore to Inverness, under construction. The photograph was taken at about the same time as the excursion from Inverness organised by John Ross visited the viaduct in July 1894.

navvies on this section were as a whole a highly respectable class of men, as respectable as could be found anywhere'. Photographs were then taken and the report continued:

> *This little operation over the holidaymakers again scrambled to their seats, and the homeward journey was commenced. The stoppages were again frequent to allow of refreshments being taken, an exceptionally long stay being made at the Craggie Inn, which was literally taken by storm. Notwithstanding the stoppages the home journey was done in four and a-half hours, and on arrival in town at 9.30 last night, the curious turnout created an enormous amount of interest, and the disembarkation at the Station Square was witnessed by a crowd which completely blocked the thoroughfare.*

The excursionists at Findhorn viaduct on 4 July 1894 after being 'picturesquely grouped and photographed' by Mr Cooper of Inverness. Murdoch MacDonald is the figure sitting on the ground cross-legged nearest the camera, and John Ross, the contractor, with beard and a stick, is seated next to him. Pipe-Major Ferguson and Piper Fraser are standing on the left holding their pipes.

It seems unlikely that William Smith took part in an excursion in which alcohol appears to have played a significant part. The Inverness Field Club excursion to the Findhorn Viaduct on the preceding 2 June would have been far more to his taste. This looked in detail at the construction of the bridge as well as the geology and history of the area. One feels, however, that the more gregarious Murdoch Macdonald enjoyed the 'novel excursion' of 4 July.

The final years on the Highland Railway

Murdoch MacDonald's correspondence for 1894–5, after the completion of the Black Isle branch, shows him working in several areas of the Highlands. In August 1894 he was at Drumnadrochit, where he was surveying the Highland Railway's route down the Great Glen to Fort William. This was in opposition to a similar line bring proposed by the North British Railway, which had just opened the West Highland line to Fort William. The following year both companies agreed to withdraw their proposed lines.

In July 1895 Murdoch MacDonald was staying at Blair Atholl and in August 1895 he was in Kingussie carrying out surveying between there and Aviemore. In both cases his work would have been in connection with the proposed doubling of the main line from Stanley to Aviemore.

Highland Railway 2–4–0 at Struan station, probably in the 1890s. This was one of the sections which Murdoch MacDonald surveyed in connection with the proposed doubling of the Stanley to Aviemore line. The stone building behind the wooden station is the Calvine Hotel.

After 1895 the correspondence in the Highland Council Archives ceases, but other sources suggest that he was later engaged in surveying a second scheme for a line to Ullapool and, possibly, a light railway from Forsinard to Portskerra. Murdoch MacDonald was involved with the extension of the railway from Strome Ferry to Kyle of Lochalsh and it was possibly through his work here that he met and married Margaret Munro, daughter of the postmaster of Lochalsh, in 1899.

By the time he married, Murdoch had left the Highland Railway, but it is not entirely clear in what year he did so. Some accounts give the date of 1896, when he set up a civil engineering practice in High Street, Inverness, while others say he resigned in 1898. On the basis of his previous activities it seems entirely possible that he might have set up his own business while still working for the HR!

An international and public service career

The Highland Railway's loss was the gain of international civil engineering. In 1898 Murdoch was appointed assistant engineer for the Aswan Dam project by Sir Benjamin Baker, consulting engineer to the Egyptian government. Sir Benjamin had been the partner of Sir John Fowler, the HR's consulting engineer, who would have heard of Murdoch MacDonald's abilities from Murdoch Paterson. Four years later he was appointed resident engineer for the dam and then in 1905 director of reservoirs in Egypt, in 1907 director of construction for the Egyptian government and in 1912 under-secretary in the Egyptian Ministry of Public Works.

A testament to Murdoch's leadership skills is the number of Highlanders who followed him to Egypt. Archibald MacCorquodale, one of his colleagues from the HR civil engineer's department, joined him almost immediately in 1899. Others from the region who came to the Aswan project included Colin Mackenzie, a journeyman mason who had worked on the Culloden viaduct, and James Fraser, formerly an engineer from the Rose Street Foundry. Murdoch is indeed reputed to have taken so many Invernessians out to Egypt that visitors noted that many Egyptians from around the Nile spoke English with an Inverness intonation.

Murdoch MacDonald was knighted in 1914. During World War One he advised the commander-in-chief, Middle East, on engineering matters and was involved with the Gallipoli campaign and the defence of the Suez Canal.

In 1921 he resigned from Egyptian government service and founded the London consulting engineering firm of MacDonald and MacCorquodale, later Sir Murdoch MacDonald and Partners. The firm carried out drainage, irrigation and hydro-electric power schemes in Britain, Spain, Portugal, Greece, Egypt, Jordan, Iraq and Pakistan.

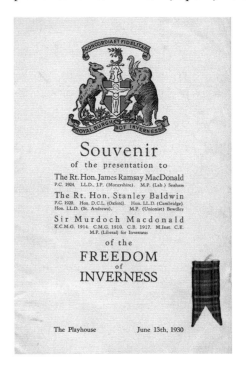

Souvenir
of the presentation to

The Rt. Hon. James Ramsay MacDonald
P.C. 1924. LL.D., J.P. (Morayshire). M.P. (Lab.) Seaham

The Rt. Hon. Stanley Baldwin
P.C. 1920. Hon. D.C.L. (Oxford). Hon. LL.D. (Cambridge).
Hon. LL.D. (St. Andrews). M.P. (Unionist) Bewdley

Sir Murdoch Macdonald
K.C.M.G. 1914. C.M.G. 1910. C.B. 1917. M.Inst. C.E.
M.P. (Liberal) for Inverness

of the

FREEDOM
of
INVERNESS

The Playhouse   June 13th, 1930

SIR MURDOCH MACDONALD, K.C.M.G., 1914; C.M.G. 1910; C.B., 1917; M.Inst.C.E.; Consulting Civil Engineer; M.P. (L.) since 1922 for Inverness District; Late Adviser and Under Secretary of State for Public Works in Egypt; Assouan Dam Protective Works and Heightening, and Isna Barrage (2nd Class Osmanieh); 2nd Class Mejidieh; Grand Officer, Order of the Nile 1915; Grand Cordon, Order of the Nile 1918; Author of article on Bridge Building, 14th edition Encycl. Britt.

Souvenir of the presentation of the freedom of Inverness to three MPs: Ramsay MacDonald, prime minister; Stanley Baldwin, opposition leader and Sir Murdoch MacDonald, the member for Inverness. Stanley Baldwin's mother was a MacDonald, so it is hardly surprising that the tartan ribbon on the souvenir was that clan's tartan. Although the three MPs represented different parties in 1930, a year later they were members of or supporters of the National Government. The detail (above) from the souvenir lists Murdoch's honours. The programme included a recording of Reginald Foort playing the *Ballet Egyptian* on the organ in recognition of the local MP's association with that country.

In 1922 Sir Murdoch was elected the Liberal MP for Inverness, a seat he retained until his retirement in 1950. The *Dictionary of National Biography* recorded that:

> *In all his elections he was returned on his personality as a distinguished Highlander, and throughout his political career his main interest was the welfare of the Highlands. His constituency stretched right across Scotland and included some of the isles, but even when he was the eldest member of the House he continued to make long journeys involved in touring his district.*

Sir Murdoch was president of the Institution of Civil Engineers and received various gold medals from engineering organisations as well as several honours from the British and Egyptian government. He was made a freeman of Inverness in 1930. He died in 1956.

The civil engineering consultancy founded in 1922 became part of Mott MacDonald, the major engineering and management consultancy. A hundred years after Murdoch MacDonald left the Highland Railway Mott MacDonald was involved in the refurbishment of some of the HR's stations as well as many other projects in Britain and abroad. When receiving the freedom of Inverness Sir Murdoch Macdonald said that he had learnt his profession 'at the feet of that first-class engineer and kindliest of men, the late Mr Murdoch Paterson.' Through the firm founded by Sir Murdoch MacDonald, the great Highland civil engineering tradition has been carried on into the 21st century.

CHAPTER 5

The Permanent Way Men
John MacDonald, Willie Duncan and Tommy Mackay

The permanent way staff or surfacemen, who were the largest group on the civil engineer's payroll, have probably received least recognition of all the different railway workers. However, their maintenance of the track and lineside was crucial to the operation of the railway. This was even more so on the Highland Railway where the line was affected by extremes of weather. Their importance was shown by the installation of telephones between permanent way men's houses and the nearest station in about 1900 so that they could be called out more quickly to deal with emergencies.

The number of men maintaining the track and their working methods changed very little during the first half of the 20th century. A general comparison between the list of permanent way staff in the 'conciliation grades' in 1911 and staff records of the early 1960s shows that the total number of staff employed in permanent way gangs was about

Permanent way staff after relaying the track over the Brown Street bridge on the approach to the Ness Viaduct in about 1930. A note on the photograph says that this was the second lot of 60ft rail laid in the district. John Chisholm, the Inverness ganger (later inspector) with white shirt stands to the left of the telegraph pole and Sandy Walker, the inspector, is the figure with tie and hands in pocket facing the camera at the far end of the bridge. Dan Kech, the lookout man, stands with his flag on the left.

A Highland Railway lookout man's badge, as worn by Dan Kech in the previous photograph. In large squads it was the job of the lookout man to warn men working on the track by sounding a horn on the approach of a train. He also carried red and green flags to stop or authorise trains to proceed during work on the line.

515 in 1911. It was only around 100 less in 1960, in spite of branch line closures and some mechanisation of working.

Willie Duncan recalls that when he became a surfaceman in 1932 the men who maintained the track were normally organised into teams of three – a foreman or ganger and two surfacemen. The area covered was usually around three to four miles. There were shorter lengths for gangs maintaining double track sections and, south of Inverness, these gangs often had a fourth member. Gangs of four also operated in other places, as, for instance, where the ganger had the additional duty of supervising relaying in the district or where a surfaceman was required to carry out ballast guard duties. There was a much bigger team of 19 based at Inverness. Four staff worked at the Inverness permanent way depot. There were also two watchmen who patrolled the cliffs west of Attadale to check for rockfalls.

The track gangs were nominally attached to stations and the stationmaster was responsible for their pay, but not for their work. For all their work on the track the gangers in the Inverness district in the 1930s reported to one of eight inspectors based at

A washout on the main line south of Millburn Junction, Inverness, on 31 May 1956. Permanent way men are preparing to unload the ballast wagons on the left. Trains continued to run through the down line on the left while the other track was being reinstated. There have been several washouts in this area over the years.

Kingussie, Aviemore, Forres, Inverness, Muir of Ord, Brora, Wick and on the Kyle line. The inspectors, in turn, reported to the chief permanent way inspector at Inverness. In HR days those reporting to the chief inspector also included permanent way inspectors at Blair Atholl (transferred to the Perth district in 1923) and at Elgin.

Until about 1934 gangers at certain locations were responsible for relaying work in the sections around them, using the local surfacemen. A separate relaying gang, which was later subdivided, was then formed. By the 1960s there were additional relaying and utility teams, the number of which changed according to the work; they were normally based at Kingussie, Inverness, Dingwall and Wick.

An indication of the responsibilities of the individual permanent way inspectors can be found in the list of those in the Forres district in 1960. Reporting to inspector Murdo Dryden were 20 gangers, a sub-ganger and 38 lengthmen based at Allanfearn, Dalcross, Gollanfield, Nairn, Auldearn, Brodie, Forres, Kinloss, Alves, Mosstowie, Burghead, Dunphail, Dava and Grantown-on-Spey.

Forres was also the site of the Highland Railway's sleeper depot, established in 1875, with a foreman and four workers. Sleepers were pressure creosoted by steam and then bored with augers for the rail chairs to be fitted by permanent way staff in the locations they were sent to. About 1934 a new building was erected and modern creosoting machinery installed. The sleepers were then sent out from Forres with the chairs already screwed on. The Forres sleeper depot closed in the late 1950s and its work transferred to the depot at Greenhill in Stirlingshire.

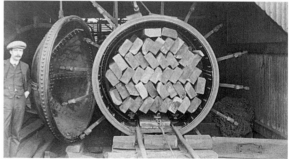

The sleeper works at Forres in 1916 showing (left) timber mounted on bogies which were then drawn into the cylinder (right) where the wood was pressure treated with creosote. These photographs were taken by R.A. Dale of the civil engineer's department, who devised the system of loading timber on to bogies.

In addition to the track gangs, there was a team of tradesmen responsible for buildings and bridges who reported to three inspectors; they in turn were responsible to the chief works inspector. In the early 1960s there were four blacksmiths, 10 carpenters, 34 masons, plasterers, slaters and labourers, 17 painters and nine plumbers. All apart from a carpenter, a mason and a labourer at Wick were based at Inverness.

At work on the track

The conditions of service for the track gangs improved greatly between the 1940s and the 1960s with a 48-hour working week of five and a half days being gradually reduced to 40 hours over five days. In the 1960s the day began at 7.40am and continued until 4.20pm in the summer and 3.56pm in the winter, with a 40-minute lunch break in each case.

One of the gang patrolled the section of line checking for any damage or disturbance to the track and rectifying any of the smaller problems, such as knocking in any of the wooden keys on the track which had become loose chairs. He then rejoined his colleagues working on maintenance jobs such as packing the ballast under the sleepers, repairing broken wires on fences, clearing drains, weeding the platforms and oiling the fishplates.

Specific jobs were undertaken at certain times of the year. In the winter the boundary fences were repaired; each gang was supplied with 100 posts, a roll of fence wire and nails and staples each year. In the early spring the lineside growth of bushes and trees was cut and burnt before it had time to grow further. In the autumn particular attention was given to improving the drainage of the ballast so that sleepers did not become waterlogged under the track joints.

Until the 1940s the majority of track on the Highland was ballasted by ash or gravel. The ash came from the locomotive depots and the gravel from the pits at Altnabreac, Rogart, Edderton, Strome Ferry, Bunchrew, Orbliston, Bowmanhill (south of Forres), Moy and Ralia (south of Newtonmore); other pits had been in use in earlier years. After World War Two the ballast was supplied from stone quarries away from the line and

Permanent way men, dealing with the aftermath of a derailment, pause from relaying damaged track while the steam breakdown crane lifts a vehicle back on to the tracks. This photograph, probably taken in the 1890s or 1900s, shows the steam crane obtained by the Highland Railway from Cowans Sheldon of Carlisle in 1886. The crane was kept in light steam in its own shed in Inverness, ready for immediate use.

taken by road lorries to loading ramps, where it was transferred to ballast hopper wagons.

The permanent way section was very labour intensive until the 1950s. Steam cranes were available for heavy relaying duties, but the men relied mainly on hand tools. The first mechanical equipment arrived in the Highlands in 1935. This was a tracked excavator which could lift a ton of gravel at a time and was transferred from pit to pit on a low well wagon.

The amount of mechanical equipment increased greatly in the 1950s and 1960s and in 1965 mobile mechanised maintenance was introduced with an increased emphasis on using road vehicles. Track gangs were amalgamated; between Inverness and Tomatin, for instance, five gangs were replaced by one. Increased mechanisation led to continuing reductions in the number of permanent way staff.

John MacDonald

The post of chief permanent way inspector on the Highland line was a responsible one and it was one John MacDonald filled with distinction for no less than 26 years up to 1941. His railway career is of particular interest because it provides a link with the navvies who built the railways in the Highlands.

In 1891, at the age of 15, John, from Newtonmore, had entered the employment of the contractor John Ross, who was building the first section of the Aviemore line to Carr Bridge. When that job was completed he moved to Ross's other contract on the line from south of Tomatin to south of Culloden Moor viaduct. Here he acted as chainman for the contractor's engineer, Pople, in measuring out the works, as well as helping to set out most of the bridges on the contract.

John MacDonald joined the Highland Railway staff in 1894 when he was offered a job with the flying squad at Kingussie, where the layout was being enlarged at the same time as the station was being rebuilt. His next post was as a lengthman at Bachan, south of Dalwhinnie, a particularly wild spot where years later the ganger, Willie Cameron, was once unable to leave his house because of the snowdrifts which had built up outside his door. When he was stationed there in 1895 John recalled that he had the worst experience of his career with snow, particularly at the notorious Black Tank cutting about 2½ miles north of Struan. He spent three months digging through snow in the area.

From 1896 John MacDonald spent the next five years on projects to increase the capacity of the main line, first working on the new loop and down platform at Killie-crankie, then in 1896 on the new crossing loops at Inchmagranachan, Moulinearn and Inchlea. Contractors made the earthworks and the HR permanent way staff laid the track. He then worked on enlarging the turntable pit and installing sidings at Blair Atholl before moving to be in charge of blasting rock for widening the line north of Struan. After the doubling of the line from Blair Atholl to Dalwhinnie was completed in 1901 John was loaned to the contractor as a ganger for a section of the new track during the six-month handover period. He was then appointed as ganger on one of the double track lengths.

In 1905 John became a permanent way inspector at Muir of Ord. He recalled his days in Ross-shire as 'happy', but also 'very busy'. In September 1908 flood damage near Bonar Bridge resulted in traffic being suspended for three days until temporary repairs could be carried out to two bridges.

A double headed train climbing up Struan bank between Garry Bridge and Dalnaspidal in the 1890s during the doubling of the line from Perth. The contractor's Scotch derricks for lifting stone are on the left. In 1899 John MacDonald was in charge of blasting at Garry Bridge during the widening of the railway there.

0–6–0 19 crosses the new steel span and stone abutments of the bridge leading to the viaduct over the River Beauly in 1909. This had replaced the original wooden bridge (see page 49). The main span of the viaduct can be seen on the left, ready to be moved into place. The rebuilding of the bridge was one of the major projects John MacDonald was involved in as permanent way inspector at Muir of Ord.

The end of December 1908 saw John MacDonald involved in clearing a snowblock between Forsinard and Georgemas. The men working on the line saw in the New Year at Forsinard, with some dancing an eightsome reel on the platform. Like William Smith and his stranded fellow passengers who had a singsong and recitations in Helmsdale station at Hogmanay 1880, this showed that Highlanders could still celebrate New Year under the most trying of circumstances!

The period from 1909 to 1911 saw John working on the rebuilding of the viaduct over the River Beauly and two new crossing loops at Fearn and Conon. This was followed by involvement in the construction of a second track between Clachnaharry and Clunes.

The rebuilding of the bridge at the east end of Bunchrew station taking place in March 1913 as part of doubling of the North Line between Clachnaharry and Bunchrew. John MacDonald was responsible for the laying of the second track on this project.

The outbreak of World War One led to the laying down of extra sidings at Dingwall, Nigg and Invergordon in 1914–15 to accommodate the extra traffic. John MacDonald's responsibilities increased in 1915 when he was appointed the Highland Railway's chief permanent way inspector. The need to provide for the increased wartime traffic included additional sidings at Kyle of Lochalsh and extra passing loops.

As well as the extra work caused by the war, there were still the consequences of floods and snowstorms to be dealt with, including the blockage of the line between Kinbrace and Wick for more than a week. John MacDonald was awarded the MBE, which was presented by the Duke of York (later George VI) for his contribution to the HR's major achievements during World War One.

The years between the end of World War One and John's retirement in 1941 were much less eventful, apart from the cloudburst north of Carr Bridge in 1923 which swept away bridges and closed the line for seven weeks. As he remarked in a retirement interview, 'the elements have been much more kind to the LMS Company than to the old Highland company'.

Drybridge station on the Portessie branch. This branch saw much permanent way activity during John MacDonald's period as chief inspector, although no trains ran over the majority of it after the line closed in 1915! The track was requisitioned by the Admiralty for use in sidings at Invergordon and Inverness Harbour and lifted in 1917. Track was relaid in 1924, and the name of Drybridge station changed to Lettefourie, but the line was never reopened and the rails were lifted again in 1937 under the supervision of Willie Duncan.

John MacDonald died in 1959. As well as recording his work on the railways and his 'upright character', the *Inverness Courier* noted that he 'drew from a remarkable memory… relating to bygone times and still followed the fortunes of the shinty and Gaelic language with enthusiasm.' Like several other Highland Railway staff mentioned in this book, he was buried in Tomnahurich cemetery in Inverness.

Willie Duncan

It was John MacDonald whom Willie Duncan was advised to approach for a job on the railways. In 1932 Willie, aged 21, from Alves in Morayshire, was working in farming and forestry, but was looking for a more secure and better paid career. John Ross, the local ganger at Alves, advised him to go to Inverness to see the chief permanent way inspector. John MacDonald looked at the prospective employee and said that he thought that Willie was 'pretty light', but that if he felt he could do the job he should see John Chisholm, the local ganger, and provide his last school report and two references from previous employers. This caused Willie no problem and one month later he travelled to Inverness on a free pass to begin his railway career.

Willie Duncan's first job was as one of 17 lengthmen working under a ganger and a sub-ganger on the Inverness section. This covered all the lines from the south end of the Ness Viaduct to the Millburn area. In addition to the maintenance of the track, they assisted in the permanent way depot by loading and unloading material and helping the blacksmiths. They also assisted the goods staff by cleaning and placing sawdust in cattle trucks and loading animals after the sheep and cattle sales at Inverness livestock markets.

The permanent way bank in Inverness in 1927. Three of the workers on the bank take a rest as they watch 'Sky Bogie' 4–4–0 14279 drift past Welsh's Bridge signal cabin. The framing behind the signal cabin was to raise the signal wires to their elevated position, clear of the feet of the men working in the yard.

During his first year in railway service Willie attended first aid training and came top of the class. John MacDonald commended him for this and it was probably because of the award that Willie received his first promotion. He was appointed a relief ballast guard after being examined in the rules of ballast train working. His first trip in his new role was on the Dornoch branch on the weed killing train which used an old locomotive tender. When acting as a ballast guard he received an extra 2s per day on top of his weekly pay of £2 3s 1d.

From 1937 to 1941 Willie recalls that his career 'went up and down like a yo-yo'. In 1937 he was placed in charge of lifting the track between Aultmore and Buckie, which had been laid down on the Keith to Portessie line in 1924, to replace that removed in World War One, but never used. He went with Willie Paterson, the district engineer, to the Keith unemployment exchange and interviewed 20 men who turned out to be 'very adaptable and formed an excellent gang'. As well as carrying out the duties of ballast guard on the tracklifting train, Willie Duncan had to supervise the men, keep charge of all material lifted, invoice the wagons, make out the timesheets and collect cash for sleepers sold on site to farmers. He was paid at an inspector's rate and received two hours overtime a week for the administrative work.

In 1938 Willie was placed in charge of a temporary gang of 20 men who were carrying out relaying and resleepering in the Muir of Ord and Kyle of Lochalsh districts. He then went back to being a lengthman at Inverness before taking over the duties of ballast guard on a regular basis when the previous guard, a reservist, was called up at the outbreak of World War Two. In 1940 Willie reverted to being a lengthman again when his predecessor returned from the forces, as did several other reservists, because of the great increase in the demands on the railways.

Willie finally ceased to be a lengthman in 1941 when he was appointed ganger at Aviemore and then in 1942 he was transferred to Dingwall as relaying ganger. This involved working over a wide section of the Highland line, notably in the Brora area, and then reinstating loops on the main line at Dalraddy and Etteridge and building a new loop at Balavil to deal with the additional wartime traffic.

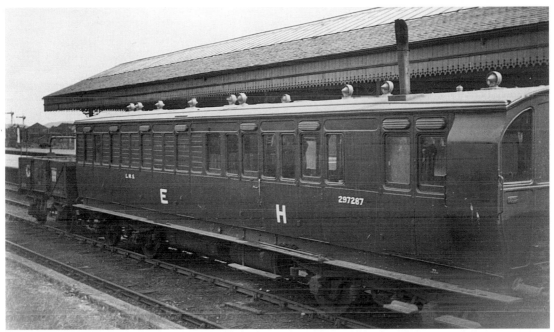

Former HR coach 13, built at Lochgorm Works in 1879, converted for departmental use by the LMS at Aviemore in 1938. Willie Duncan slept in a similar coach at Aviemore when he was ganger there and unable to find a house. He recalls that his method of central heating was two hot bricks in his bed on a cold night.

The accommodation for the relaying gang was in two departmental coaches, one used as a dormitory and the other for eating. Tommy Mackay, who was one of the gang when they were working on the main line, recalls that Willie was always up first, cooking breakfast so that a prompt start could be made at 7.20am. The men worked through to noon, when they had a hour's break for lunch, and then again from 1pm to 5pm. It was demanding work that sometimes involved relaying a 60ft length of rail in the 20 minutes that was available between trains. Tommy added that they slept well at night!

By 1943 Willie's abilities must have been clear to his bosses in Inverness and in that year he was appointed assistant to the chief permanent way inspector at Inverness. In this post he gained valuable experience in stock keeping, book keeping, making out returns and ordering material. In 1945 he was appointed permanent way inspector at Kingussie, returning to Inverness as inspector there in 1955.

In 1959 Willie Duncan was appointed chief permanent way inspector at Inverness. His area of responsibility was extended in 1965 with the setting up of the Highland Lines organisation, which also included the section of the main line from Struan to Stanley that

Willie Duncan (third from left, back row) at the first-ever course held for permanent way inspectors at the School of Transport, Derby, in September 1948. Willie was one of four inspectors from the Scottish Region selected to attend. Because of the distance involved he was unable to return home at the weekends during the four-week course.

The Inverness civil engineering staff and permanent way inspectors in 1950. Standing, from left to right, are: Alec MacDonald, staff clerk, Sam Campbell, chief clerk, Malcom Murchison, engineer, Willie Fraser, Alec MacDonald, Angus MacTavish, Alec Nicholson and John Alison, all inspectors, and Willie Noble, assistant to the chief inspector. Seated from left to right are Alistair Geikie, engineer, Willie Duncan and Bob Mackintosh, both inspectors, Archie Mackintosh, district engineer, Alec MacDonald, chief inspector, John Chisholm, inspector, and Tommy Campbell, assistant district engineer. The occasion was the presentation of the inspector's cup, which went to the inspector with the highest maintained section of track. On this occasion it was won by Bob Mackintosh, responsible for the Kyle line.

had been transferred to the Perth district in 1923, as well as the former Great North of Scotland Railway lines west of Inverurie.

The post of chief permanent way inspector involved much work out on the line, particularly in the aftermath of snow, floods, washouts and accidents. Willie's worst experience with snow came on 9 February 1963. Three days earlier a passenger train had been trapped between Dava and Dunphail. The train had been freed, but the Forres to Aviemore line had again become blocked at Dava Moor. Steam had now disappeared from the Highlands and two diesel locomotives were sent out between two of the recently introduced independent snowploughs. One of these was a converted locomotive tender and the other was a purpose-built unit built on top of a tender frame.

On arrival, via Forres, at the blockage at Dava, where the drifts were as high as 13 feet, Willie advised that the drift should be charged. He held tightly on to the handrails in the cab of the leading diesel, as John MacDonald had told him to on a steam locomotive when he was a ballast guard on snow clearance duties. This was just as well, because the converted tender overturned and it and the two locomotives also became derailed. The snowplough was moved off the track and the locomotives rerailed. Clearing the line was then resumed from the Aviemore end with the purpose-built snowplough while a mechanical digger was used at the Forres end. A week after the line had been cleared, however, two engines patrolling the line to clear it of snow became snowed in near Dava summit. They were not recovered for a fortnight as priority had to be give to clearing the main line, where a freight train had become blocked at Dalwhinnie.

The overturned snowplough, which had been converted from a LNER locomotive tender, at Dava on 9 February 1963, with the two derailed diesel locomotives behind. A snow fence can be seen on the extreme left; it had proved of limited value during the preceding blizzard.

The most difficult job in Willie Duncan's career was dealing with the aftermath of the derailment of two wagons of coal between Dalwhinnie and Newtonmore on 17 June 1975. The two wagons were pulled along in the goods train damaging almost eight miles of track. Several hundred rail chairs were replaced and a speed limit of 10mph introduced. It was decided that six miles of track had to be replaced with continuous welded rail and the ballast cleaned.

In 1967 the Highland Lines structure was abolished and Willie became district inspector for the area from Inverness to Golspie. By now the civil engineering for the Highlands was controlled from Perth, and it was there that Willie Duncan moved in 1970 when he became chief permanent way inspector again, this time for all railways north of Dunblane and Leuchars. He retired in 1975.

Thirty years after leaving the railways Willie is still recalled as 'a first-class permanent way man' and 'firm but fair' by those who worked

A crane lifting the brake van clear after a ballast train became derailed south of Tain on 21 June 1969. After accidents such as this Willie Duncan had to deal with the rapid re-laying of damaged track.

for him or knew him. Things were usually tightened up after he took charge of a section and there was certainly less playing of cards by some permanent way gangs. One gang even bored a spyhole in the side of their cabin so they could keep an eye out for his approach and cut any breaks short before his arrival!

Today Willie Duncan still leads an active retirement in Inverness looking after his garden and taking charge of coach trips for his fellow senior citizens. In 1991 he read an excellent paper on his career to the Permanent Way Institute, which was later published in their *Journal* and for which he was presented with a picture of the Summer Isles which hangs in his home today. His paper is an invaluable record of the conditions and work of permanent way staff and has formed the basis for much of this chapter.

Willie Duncan in 2004 holding the 'best first aid pupil' medal he received in 1931.

Tommy Mackay

John MacDonald and Willie Duncan were the only members of their family who worked on the railway. Tommy Mackay had a father and two brothers who also worked for the London, Midland and Scottish Railway. Tommy's father, George, who was a farmer's son from Easter Ross, had started life as a fisherman in Sutherland before joining the permanent way staff at

Strome Ferry in 1925 and then moving to the railway cottages half a mile west of Attadale on the Kyle line in 1934. Donald, one of Tommy's brothers, was an engine driver, first at Kyle and then at Ayr and in London, and his other brother, George, was a clerk at Strathcarron station.

After starting work on the relaying gang under Willie Duncan in 1942, when it was based at Kingussie, Tommy moved back to Attadale in 1946 to join his father on the Kyle line. While Tommy was a lengthman, his father's job was purely as a watchman on the section of line west of Attadale, where he had to check for possible rockfalls from the cliffs above Loch Carron obstructing the line. There were two huts with phones to report any falls from the cliff.

When Tommy moved to the Kyle line he worked on the Strathcarron to Kyle gang. This was one of four long sections that had been created in 1934 when motorised trolley working had been introduced on the Kyle and North lines. Motor trolleys seating 10 men and trailers with tools meant larger gangs of men could deal with jobs on the line more quickly. The trolleys were taken on and off the line by a small turntable to allow trains to pass, though the working time was sometimes reduced when the driver was waiting for the token before the trolley could be put back on to the track. This was one of the factors which led to the abolition of the motorised system and the reversion to smaller gangs in 1948.

When the motorised trolley system was in operation Tommy would be picked up and dropped from the trolley outside the permanent way men's cottages. After 1948 he worked as a lengthman in a team of three men on the five-mile length centred on Attadale station. In 1960 he became the ganger for the section and three years later was appointed permanent way inspector for the Kyle line.

Attadale with the station shelter built by the railway carpenters in Inverness and assembled at Attadale shortly before this photograph was taken in 1954. It eventually blew down after lack of maintenance. The platform had once held the original larger station building, the stationmaster's house and a signal cabin. In the 1950s and 1960s a red flag was kept in the shelter for passengers to stop trains.

The 1960s and early 1970s were years of great uncertainty for the line to Kyle of Lochalsh. It was one of the lines proposed for closure under the Beeching cuts, but the proposal was rejected largely because of the extremely poor alternative road connections to Kyle. By 1971, however, a new road running from Strathcarron through Attadale to Strome Ferry parallel to the railway was nearing completion and the diversion of the Stornaway ferry service to Ullapool from 1973 had been announced. The Government therefore agreed to the closure of the Kyle line at the end of 1973.

The construction of the road brought problems for Tommy Mackay. The railway had to be moved on to a new embankment in Loch Carron as the road was on the landward side. Blasting of the cliff face was also necessary to create space for the road in some areas. The unstable nature of the rocks resulted in two landslides in the area where the railway stationed watchmen. The landslides closed the line for six weeks in May and June 1969 and for 17 weeks from November 1969 to March 1970. Tommy was in charge of clearing the line on both occasions. As a result of the landslides an avalanche shelter was constructed for road and railway west of Attadale and steel mesh placed over the adjoining cliff face.

The railway track through the avalanche shelter has had a longer life than might have been hoped when it was constructed. The line was reprieved for a further year in 1973 and then permanently when it was decided to establish a yard for building concrete oil platforms at Loch Kishorn near the mouth of Loch Carron. Construction material for this was brought by rail to Strome Ferry for onward transport across Loch Carron. New sidings had to be laid at Strome in 1975 for this and Tommy supervised their construction.

The avalanche shelter west of Attadale, photographed from a train in 1981. The road is covered by the left-hand section of the shelter.

Tommy Mackay (far left) and the permanent way squads from the west end of the Kyle line laying track in the sidings at Strome Ferry in 1975 for offloading the construction material for the Kishorn oil platform yard.

Tommy Mackay was made redundant in 1981, but he continues to live in the railway cottages west of Attadale, which he purchased and converted to one dwelling. Every week he travels to Dingwall over the line with which his family was associated for so many years.

Tommy Mackay standing on the opposite side of the Kyle railway from his cottage at Attadale. This was originally built as two cottages for the permanent way staff.

CHAPTER 6

Two Victorian Guards
William Hood and Donald Campbell

When John Edgar Campbell wrote *The Iron Track Through the Highlands* in 1922 he devoted two chapters to HR guards, for as he stated:

> *The guards were among the most interesting of the old-time railway employees. There was a large staff of these officials – passengers and goods – and each was in himself an important personage. The passenger guard was at that time perhaps one of the best known and most popular men in the Highlands as he moved up and down the country day in day out, making the way smooth for the travelling public, while he acted in the capacity of their guide, philosopher and friend...*

Two of the well known guards were William Hood and Donald Campbell, whose careers are described in this chapter.

Donald Campbell (1845–1911) photographed towards the beginning and end of his 40-year career as a guard. His obituary in 1911 described him as 'one of the oldest and most highly esteemed guards on the Highland Railway'.

The role of the guard in dealing with passengers was greater in the earlier years of the Highland Railway because of the limited facilities in coaches. The normal HR coaches were built without lavatories until the 1880s, when they were provided for first-class passengers. This resulted in the HR deciding to install urinals on both platforms at a number of passing places in 1876. In addition, as restaurant facilities were not available until a Pullman car was introduced to Aviemore in 1922, longer stops were made at Kingussie, Bonar Bridge and Achnasheen so that passengers could use the refreshment facilities there. Ensuring that all the passengers were back on board the train, so that it could leave on time, was therefore a significant part of the guard's duties.

Less obviously, but more importantly, the guard was responsible for the safe operation of his train. This could be an onerous job before the installation of the automatic vacuum brake on Highland coaches, which began in the 1880s. Until then the HR fitted its coaches with Newall's mechanical brakes. A wheel and ratchet in the guard's van freed the brake blocks on the adjacent coaches through a complicated mechanism of rods and mechanical couplings; releasing the ratchet applied the brakes. This had to be done manually by the guard each time the train stopped. On longer trains the guard applied the brakes on one or two coaches and the brakesman on a further one or two.

In the Victorian period the guard not only had to cope with a manual form of braking, but also had to work a large number of mixed trains. In these trains the wagons without

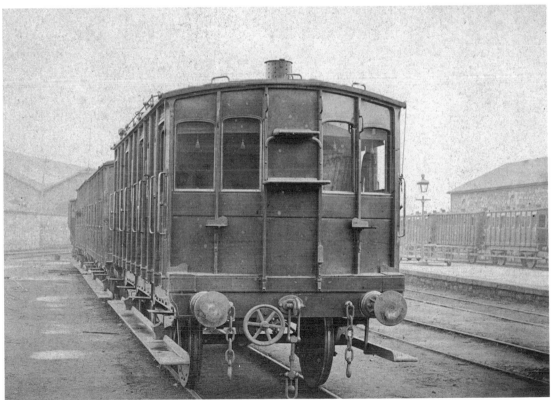

Four-wheel first-class coupé carriage built in 1873 at Inverness. This shows the wheel used to apply the Newall mechanical brake after it had been shunted into a siding. On the roof can be seen one of the ventilated cylinders into which were dropped the oil lamps for lighting the carriages.

any continuous brakes were placed in front of the passenger coaches so that they could be more easily shunted into the goods sidings at stations. Several accidents took place when couplings broke between wagons and coaches while the train was climbing gradients or when carriages were inadvertently set in motion during shunting operations. As John Thomas relates in *The Skye Line* there were several incidents on the steep gradients of the line west from Dingwall in the 1890s when the HR was continuing to marshal wagons in front of coaches in defiance of Board of Trade regulations. It was only after a particularly serious runaway of coaches down the bank from Achterneed in 1897, and a change of general manager, that the HR decided to comply with the Regulation of Railways Act of 1889. Fifty trains became passenger only and additional goods trains were introduced.

A mixed passenger and goods train headed by Skye Bogie 4–4–0 85 at Kyle of Lochalsh station soon after its opening in 1897. The train is marshalled with the coaches at the front and goods wagons behind. This was the order that the Board of Trade specified, but the Highland Railway had ignored until the early 1890s.

When a Newall's brake was in use a brakesman assisted the guard on most HR trains as detailed above. In the late 1870s, for instance, Donald Tulloch, who was one of the guards on the mail trains to Wick, had Colin Mackay as his regular brakesman. Mackay was later to become the stationmaster at Inverness. After the introduction of automatic continuous brakes, trains on the Perth line still continued to carry two guards, as did goods and mixed trains.

In the 1860s the guards worked a 50-hour week. When in 1866 through carriages were introduced between Perth and Bonar Bridge, Perth guards worked through with them on a journey of about nine hours. After a petition was received from the guards, the HR board agreed to pay for a room for them in the inn adjacent to Bonar Bridge station, if no other place could be got. In the summer they were presumably expected to sleep in the coaches.

William Hood

The Highland guards became particularly well known to passengers because they usually worked on specific trains. One of the best known was William Hood, who joined the Inverness and Aberdeen Junction Railway as a porter at Elgin in 1858. A year later he became a lamp man, responsible for the oil lamps which were placed into the carriage roofs, and then he became a brakesman on Inverness to Keith trains before being promoted to guard.

Hood was the guard on the first through train from Inverness to Perth on 9 September 1863, which journey, he later recalled, took two days. This was because the line had been opened without the opportunity for the locomotive drivers to learn the route or the station clerks to be trained in working telegraph instruments. In addition, not all the water columns for the locomotive had been installed and water had to be taken from burns on the Struan bank. From 1863 William Hood became a regular guard on the 'Perth Road'. He was the guard on the royal trains for Queen Victoria and the Prince of Wales (later Edward VII) on several occasions.

One of the Inverness and Aberdeen Junction brake vans which William Hood travelled in on the first train between Inverness and Perth in 1863. It was photographed in the 1900s when it was still in departmental use at Perth and was seen as being of historical interest. The rails for carrying luggage on the roof can be seen. The small open door on the left was for the ventilated locker in which dogs were carried.

One of the duties of guards was to deal with luggage, which could be very considerable in the case of those travelling to shooting lodges. In the late 1860s luggage was often carried on the roofs of carriages rather than in the luggage van. William Hood was adjusting luggage on the roof of a carriage on a particularly busy day when he was struck by an overhead bridge. He was injured, but fortunately survived the accident.

Like many other Highland employees, William Hood had memorable experiences dealing with the 'storm king' of snow. In the early 1880s he was guard on a mixed train of passenger, livestock and fish vehicles for Perth which was snowed up north of Dava for several days. He managed to lead his passengers to safety at Dava station, where passengers from an Inverness train trapped south of the station joined them. Food was obviously in short supply and Hood telegraphed for permission to use fish from the trucks on his train. The cattle in the five wagons travelling from Easter Ross to Smithfield market all perished.

In the mid-1880s William Hood lost the sight in his right eye as a result of an accident when the train on which he was the guard broke in two on Struan Bank. This showed that the methods of operation of trains on the HR at that time, mentioned above, could make the guard's job a dangerous one at times.

Engraving from a contemporary weekly periodical of one of the snowblocks at Dava in the early 1880s. This shows the conditions in which William Hood's train was marooned.

Following the accident Hood had to leave his job as a guard. His regular passengers and colleagues on the Perth route presented him with a purse of gold as a farewell gift. He then took up shunting duties at Inverness until 1909 when he was well over 70. On his retirement from that post he was presented with another purse of sovereigns and a clock at an event which was attended by Thomas Wilson, the HR general manager, and several Inverness town councillors.

Donald Campbell

One of William Hood's colleagues on the 'Perth Road' was Donald Campbell. Donald, the son of a meal dealer, was born in Ardesier in 1845. He appears to have joined the Highland Railway as a marshalman (shunter) at Inverness in 1864. Three years later he married Christina McIver, who had been a lady's maid to Baroness Burdett-Coutts, the philanthropist, in London.

Donald Campbell progressed to become a guard by the early 1870s and was one of the select group who accompanied the HR through coaches from Inverness to

Donald Campbell flagging off his train from Kincraig, where he has been speaking to stationmaster Peter Wilkie, about 1900.

Glasgow. The Highland and Caledonian Railways provided these through coaches on alternate days. South of Perth, the Highland guard appears to have been in charge of the train for at least part of the journey.

John Edgar Campbell wrote that 'Danny' Campbell was as well known at Buchanan Street station (the Caledonian's terminus for the north in Glasgow) as in Inverness. Like James Dunbar, another guard who regularly worked through to Glasgow, he was a welcome sight to exiles from the Highlands in the Lowland city when he stayed overnight.

By the time Donald Campbell reached 60 he no longer worked to Glasgow. A list of guards working in October 1905 shows that he was the guard on the 8.40am from

An Inverness to Perth train headed by 4–6–0 *Ballindalloch Castle* at Aviemore in the early 1900s. The front three vehicles are North British Railway coaches for Edinburgh and the coaches immediately behind are Highland Railway carriages for Glasgow. At Aviemore a through coach for Edinburgh from the Forres route was probably being added. Multi-portion trains were one of the features of the Inverness-Perth route which guards had to deal with.

Inverness to Perth and then on the 4.10pm from Perth to Inverness, arriving back at 8.35pm. The second guard on this duty was Donald Macdonald. On alternate days Donald exchanged duties with Alexander Ramsay, working the 7.50am from Inverness to Tain and returning on the 10.00am from Tain which reached Inverness at 12 noon. The Tain duty appears to have been a less onerous one allocated to the older HR guards.

Donald Campbell was still working as a guard when he died in 1911. His obituary,

Donald Campbell with his wife and family about 1900. Both his sons were HR clerks at this time. Seated is John, whose career is described in the next chapter. Alexander, the younger son, who is standing, emigrated in 1900 to pursue his railway career in Canada.

reflecting the bond that was built up between guards and their regular travellers, stated that: 'His courteous and kindly disposition made him a favourite with the travelling public.'

By 1911 the guard's job had become easier than in the earlier days of William Hood and Donald Campbell, when in J.E. Campbell's words:

> *A single line with steep gradients liable at various points to be blocked by flooding, wash-a-ways, landslides and snowdrifts, and worked by an antiquated block system certainly called for the exercise of no ordinary amount of care on the part of those responsible for the trains...*

CHAPTER 7

Clerks to Stationmasters
John and Bert Campbell

All but the smallest stations on the Highland Railway were under the charge of a stationmaster or agent. Stationmasters started their careers as clerks, or possibly as porters, and worked at different stations in more senior roles before their first appointment in charge of a station. They could then expect to move on to take charge of larger stations.

The clerk's job may have been the first step on the ladder to possibly becoming a stationmaster, but it was nevertheless a responsible one. It involved handling cash for tickets, all of which were individually numbered, and also for excess baggage and luggage sent in advance of travel. The clerk had also to know what route to book passengers on and be ready to provide timetable information to enquirers.

Other duties included weighing, charging for, labelling and recording parcels and

Tickets issued at Culloden Moor station in 1909 and at Pitlochry in 1960. The only significant change in format is that the Pitlochry ticket has been dated on the back. The handwritten alteration on the 1960 ticket shows the extra work for clerks because of pre-printed fares which later increased.

Label fixed to luggage for which an excess charge had been paid at the originating station. First-class passengers could take luggage weighing 120lb free, and third-class passengers 100lb. Certain items, such as prams, were not counted as luggage and had to be paid for separately.

(A. 476)
THE HIGHLAND RAILWAY.

EXCESS LUGGAGE—PAID

FROM

_____Station,_____Train,

_____19____ ____Packages.

Highland Railway newspaper label of the late 1860s. There were also labels for parcels.

weighing and dealing with any excess charges for passengers' luggage. There was also much paperwork relating to goods traffic, such as consignment notes, invoices and statements for goods unclaimed. Returns had to be made to the HR headquarters and split into that purely on the HR and that going on to other railways. This was so that the receipts could be divided between the different companies. Passenger receipts were similarly divided.

In addition to selling tickets and dealing with paperwork the clerks were expected to be on the platform to collect tickets from passengers alighting from trains. For this they put on a company cap. The HR Board turned down a request that clerks should be provided with suits or uniforms by the company in 1878.

Clerks also had to learn how to work the telegraph system, as this was how stations communicated with one another and with Inverness on a day-to-day basis. Until the 1940s the telegraph was also an essential part of the operation of the Highland system.

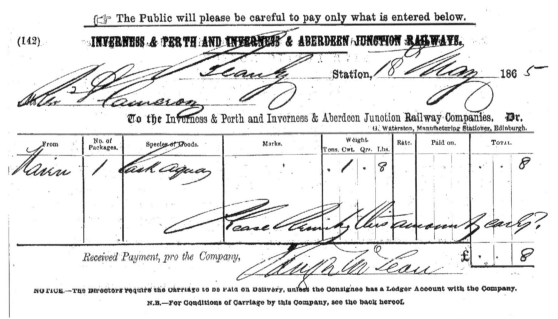

Invoice issued in May 1865, shortly before the Inverness & Perth and the Inverness & Aberdeen Railways amalgamated to become the Highland Railway.

The porter's job did not require the same clerical skills as the clerk's, but it was also a varied one. The porters had to meet every passenger train and load and unload luggage and parcels as well as helping passengers to alight. They had to keep the station tidy and maintain and light the oil lamps. At most stations the porters also had to deal with goods traffic, although the largest stations had porters specifically allocated to passengers and others to freight. The goods duties included putting labels on wagons, tying ropes and covers on open wagons and helping to load sheep and cattle into livestock wagons. Any

Summary of parcels and miscellaneous traffic from Killiecrankie passing over the Caledonian Railway to Glasgow. This is but one example of the paperwork which had to be completed by the station's staff.

Form for a telegraph sent in 1881.

empty livestock wagons had to be cleaned out and disinfected with lime wash and the floor covered with sawdust before they could be used again.

At some less important stations the stationmaster himself had to carry out all these duties without the help of any clerks or porters, but he would be assisted by a pointsman who worked the signal cabin. This was the case between Helmsdale and Georgemas, where there were only four trains a day. A few very small stations, particularly those on the Dornoch, Lybster and Portessie branches, had only a stationmaster.

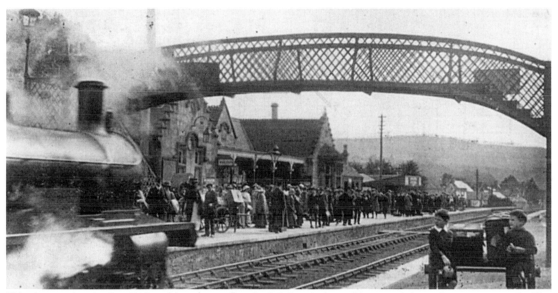

Pitlochry station in the 1900s with a Jones Goods 4–6–0 entering with a south-bound passenger train. The number of passengers on the platform is a reminder that in the more populous areas of the Highlands station staff had to deal with large numbers of people when trains were due.

At the smaller stations there were periods when the stationmaster had to operate the signal cabins. At most stations he might be called upon to do so in case of an emergency or to help when trains crossed and delay might be caused by the pointsman having to go to both signal cabins and deal with the single line tablet.

At the larger stations the stationmaster might carry out fewer varied duties, but had to supervise a number of staff, not only clerks and porters, but also signal staff, pointsmen and gatekeepers (employed at level crossings) and a cleaner.

The skills that were required of a stationmaster were therefore wide ranging. He was responsible for the smooth running of the station and in particular for its cash. Staff from the auditor's section would turn up unannounced and query any anomalies or common, but frowned on, practices such as maintaining a 'float' of any spare coppers left after balancing up the takings in order to meet any shortfall which might occur in the following days.

The stationmaster was expected to deal courteously with all his passengers. If one of the landowners was upset by his treatment at a station, he could complain directly to Inverness. The stationmaster had also to identify and secure potential traffic, especially in areas where the Highland and Great North of Scotland Railways had competing lines.

4–4–0 T58 *Burghead* at the original station at Burghead in the 1880s. The stationmaster, with top hat, stands in the centre of the group. Stationmasters appear to have worn top hats into the 1890s, although the HR decided to issue them with caps in 1871. By the 1920s only the stationmaster at Inverness wore a top hat.

```
C/_____
   3260.

      Chas. Lamond,                    Mr. Wilkie,

Accountant, Highland Railway,             Agent,

     Inverness, 14th Octr.  03.          Alness.


         Railway Passengers' Assurance.
         ─────────────────────────

     Your total remittance for 2nd inst: was £3, and the

whole of this amount is shown on your Cash Note as for

Passenger Traffic.  I cannot find the 3d. shown on any of

your Cash Notes for this month up to date.  Please note

and remit the amount without further delay.
```

This memorandum from the accountant's department to the stationmaster at Alness in 1903 shows that station accounts had to be accurate down to the last few pennies.

A very important public official

In *The Iron Track Through the Highlands* John Edgar Campbell described the Highland stationmaster as 'a very important public official'. The stationmaster ranked alongside positions such as the minister, doctor, schoolmaster and factor of the local estate as a leading member of the community. The title 'agent' was sometimes used instead of 'stationmaster', particularly in the 1900s. This reflected a certain status as it was also used for the manager of local branches of the Scottish banks, who was often responsible for the bank in addition to his solicitor's business.

The stationmaster would often be involved in one of the local churches and other local organisations. John Kinnaird, the stationmaster at Birnam and Dunkeld, for instance, took the lead in establishing the Birnam Institute, which provided a library, reading, refreshment and recreation rooms, and a public hall for the local community.

The minister and elders of St Andrew's, Aviemore, in the 1960s. Bert Campbell, stationmaster at Aviemore, stands on the far right. Stationmasters frequently played a leading part in church and other community affairs. The other elders include two locomotive drivers.

John Kinnaird was also involved with the commercial life of the local community in ways that fell outside the Highland Railway's wishes. In 1873, following protests by local traders in Perthshire, stationmasters were forbidden to deal in coal, lime, potatoes and manure to the detriment of the traders.

A similar complaint was made in 1879 and stationmasters were again told to discontinue trading 'directly or indirectly'. James Kinnaird certainly continued indirect trading because Beatrix Potter, who spent several holidays in the Dunkeld area, wrote in her diary in 1892 that:

> His brother Mr James Kinnaird... sits in a zinc shed labelled 'Manures And Feeding Stuff', coals being discreetly in the background. It need hardly be said that Mr James is but a cover or blind for Mr John.

The HR board in 1888 specifically reprimanded John Kinnaird for letting out houses and he was forbidden to act beyond his 'regular duties'. Four years later, however, Beatrix Potter records him letting a house to her father for the summer, on behalf of its owner.

A group of station staff at Birnam and Dunkeld in 1898. John Kinnaird who had retired as stationmaster a year earlier is seated on the far right, with the local minister and the stationmaster next to him. John Campbell, then a goods clerk at the station, stands fifth from the left.

John Kinnaird was by no means alone in trading on his own behalf. Some stationmasters resigned their posts to concentrate on their commercial concerns. William Paterson, the first stationmaster at Dingwall in 1862, traded in coal, grain and other commodities, and later resigned from the railway to build up what his obituary in the *Highland News* in 1909 described as a 'very extensive business'.

John Lawrence, the stationmaster at Aviemore, was another who built up his own thriving business. He ran not only a general merchant's store, but also the local post office. When a new building was constructed for his shop, he also included a villa for letting to visitors. In the 1900s John Lawrence retired from the railway, but continued to run his business and could now do so under his own rather than his family's name.

There were occasions when HR staff were allowed to carry out work additional to their railway duties. Stationmasters could sell coal at country stations where they would not compete with any railway customers.

In addition certain stations also housed the local post and telegraph office. The stationmaster was paid an additional salary for this and, as a result, was often reluctant to move to another station without a post office, even though he might have been paid a higher basic salary.

John Campbell

John Campbell's father Donald was a long-serving employee of the Highland Railway (see Chapter 5), but John had still to pass the HR's own examination to become a clerk. He sat the paper at the Highland office on 18 November 1892, when he was 17. Three days later Andrew Dougall, the general manager, notified him that he had been successful and he was asked to provide a medical certificate and a certificate of character from his last schoolteacher.

On 29 December 1892 John Campbell received a further letter saying that he had been appointed apprentice clerk in the goods manager's office at Inverness at a salary of £20 for the first year, £25 for the second year and £30 for the third and last year. A payment for the superannuation fund was deducted from the salary. He had to sign a legal agreement which committed him to serve the HR for three years and which indemnified the company against any 'loss, damage, and expense' incurred as result of 'his omissions or defaults'. His father had to act as surety for the agreement. It was signed in April 1893, by which time John Campbell had begun a lifelong railway career, as shown by the list of his other appointments:

29 December	1892	*Apprentice Clerk*	*Goods Manager's Office, Inverness*
19 August	1895	*Goods Clerk*	*Keith*
14 September	1896	*Goods Clerk*	*Boat of Garten*
16 March	1898	*Goods Clerk*	*Birnam and Dunkeld*
11 May	1899	*Goods Clerk*	*Burghead*
13 May	1900	*Chief Goods Clerk*	*Thurso*
23 November	1900	*Goods Clerk*	*Kyle of Lochalsh*
6 December	1900	*Chief Goods Clerk*	*Aberfeldy*
12 November	1901	*Relief Clerk (and Stationmaster)*	*Inverness*
5 March	1907	*Stationmaster*	*Lairg*
28 April	1914	*Stationmaster*	*Strathpeffer*
13 August	1917	*Stationmaster*	*Aviemore*
19 March	1926	*Died*	

After he had completed his apprenticeship in the goods manager's office, John Campbell moved in 1895 to the first of a number of posts as a goods clerk at different stations which, as the list shows, took him to the extremities of the HR system at Keith, Birnam and Dunkeld, Thurso and Kyle of Lochalsh. These were more geographically spread postings than was normally the case and possibly suggested that he was being given wide experience as someone who would progress relatively quickly to becoming a stationmaster.

4–4–0 130 *Loch Fannich* with a passenger train at Thurso in August 1923. On the right is a vacuum brake-fitted wagon for carrying barrels of fish south. When John Campbell was chief goods clerk at Thurso he dealt with much fish traffic.

A. 440 **THE HIGHLAND RAILWAY.**

PERISHABLE GOODS.

FISH—PER GOODS TRAIN.

From KYLE OF LOCHALSH

TO BROAD STREET, L & N.W.

Via DUNKELD and CAL., CARLISLE, and L & N.W.

Date_____191_ Wagon No. _____

Owner and No. on Sheet,_____

Barrel label for the regular traffic of fish from Kyle of Lochalsh to London, via the Caledonian and London and North Western Railways. John Campbell worked at Kyle for a fortnight in between his appointments at Thurso and Aberfeldy.

John Campbell would certainly have gained varied experience from his postings. At Keith and Boat of Garten he would have dealt with traffic coming off the Great North of Scotland Railway. At Thurso and Kyle there were fish to be loaded from the local fleet and at Kyle there was also the traffic from the MacBrayne's steamers from the Western Isles. At Aberfeldy there was the whisky traffic from the local distillery and and at all stations there was the general goods and livestock traffic.

The move to being a goods clerk at Kyle of Lochalsh in November 1900 after being chief goods clerk at Thurso for six months might appear to be a step down, but this was not the case. The Thurso appointment was a temporary one, while the permanent chief clerk was acting as a relief stationmaster to cover staff leave or long-term illness. From November 1901 John Campbell himself acted as a relief clerk based in Inverness and, although not formally recorded on his appointments, documents and photographs show that he was also a relief stationmaster at Fochabers in 1903.

In March 1907 John Campbell gained his first permanent post as stationmaster when he was appointed to Lairg. The following month he married Helen Munro, a milliner from Aberfeldy, in the Salutation Hotel, Perth. Their family, which was to comprise twin sons, Bert and John, and two daughters, Chrissie and Vera, grew up in various station houses.

Lairg was one of the busier stations on the line to Wick. A significant amount of mail and other traffic arrived at the station for the large hinterland of Sutherland it served. Once a year there were also many extra trains to be run from the sheep sale at Lairg, the largest in Scotland. The pens were adjacent to the station. At Lairg John Campbell operated a coal business which the stationmaster was permitted to do there.

In April 1914 John Campbell and his family moved to Strathpeffer. This was an important station on the system. In 1911 the Railway had opened a new 90-bed hotel,

The staff at Fochabers Town station in 1903 at the time when John Campbell (far right) was acting stationmaster. The other staff are the porter, pointsman, guard for the branch train to Orbliston Junction and clerk.

John Campbell and the station staff at Lairg in about 1910. The main station buildings in the right background are in the cottage style favoured by the Sutherland Railway.

Aerial view of Lairg station in the 1950s. The oil depot, which was in its infancy during John Campbell's time, has grown greatly, but little else has changed since the 1900s. The pens for the sheep sales can be seen on the lower right. The stationmaster's house is at right angles to the main station buildings.

the Highland Hotel, aimed at those coming to 'take the waters' at the Highland Spa as well as holidaymakers wishing to take advantage of the 'bracing air' and the excellent golf course. On Tuesdays in the summer the HR ran a through train from Aviemore to Strathpeffer which bypassed Inverness.

John Campbell had, however, only a few months to deal with the tourist traffic in Strathpeffer before this declined after the outbreak of World War One in August 1914. The Highland Hotel was requisitioned for military use and in July 1916 Inverness and the country to the north were declared a restricted area; all passengers entering the area had to have an identity card or permit.

In August 1917 John Campbell was promoted to be stationmaster at Aviemore, the largest HR station outside Inverness. Here he succeeded Thomas Fraser, who was reduced to being goods foreman at Forres after embezzling money from the railway.

The wartime traffic at Aviemore not only involved the vastly increased wartime traffic passing through to the North, but also timber being loaded from the local forests, mainly for pit props.

Although the heavy wartime traffic declined after 1918, Aviemore continued to be a very busy station throughout the final HR years and into the period of LMS ownership from 1923. Passenger trains for the Carr Bridge and Forres routes were divided and joined. Empty cups were collected from trains from the south and returned to the Kingussie refreshment rooms, and in the winter, footwarmers were replaced.

Aviemore proved to be John Campbell's last posting as he died suddenly in March

Postcard of the Station Hotel at Aviemore, which was built after the station became a junction in 1898, the period when Aviemore developed greatly from a settlement of a few houses. The hotel had its own electricity generator which also supplied the station house.

Helen Campbell outside the station house in Aviemore in about 1920, when her husband, John, was stationmaster there. In the left background can be seen the wooden 'summer house' where the family lived when the station house was let out during the holiday period. It was common practice to let out station houses, with the let being in the stationmaster's wife's name to avoid HR disapproval of these arrangements.

John Campbell (centre) with station clerks (seated) and a signalman, goods guard, relief signalman and passenger guard (standing) at Aviemore in 1925. John disliked the new uniforms introduced by the LMS, which are shown here; he preferred the longer HR stationmaster's jacket.

1926 aged 51. The Campbell tradition of working on the railway was, however, to be continued for a further generation by his son, Bert.

Bert Campbell

Bert Campbell was the name by which one of John's twin sons, christened Robert, was known. He was born in 1911 and had helped his father by filling and collecting money from chocolate machines and doing other odd jobs round Strathpeffer and Aviemore stations while still a small boy. He also made himself useful at Kingussie station by folding the covers for wagons and cleaning trucks when waiting for his train back to Aviemore after his day at Kingussie High School.

After his father's death Bert was promised a post by the LMS and started work as a clerk at Boat of Garten in April 1927. Like his father

Twins Bert (right) and John Campbell, photographed soon after their birth in 1911 outside the station house in Lairg where their father, John, was stationmaster. Bert was to have a long and distinguished career on railways in the Highlands.

he had to pass the clerk's examination before starting work and had a second examination on railway working when he reached 18. His salary for his first year was £35, the second year £45 and the third year £55. This was £15 more than his father had started on in 1892 and with annual increases for the next two years of his apprenticeship of £10 rather than £5. The rate of pay for apprentice or junior clerks had increased less than for some other grades and, after payment of national insurance, unemployment and superannuation fund contributions, was certainly not a generous salary.

Bert recalls that junior porters, who were paid wages at an hourly rate, earned a few shillings more each week than clerks who were on a fixed annual salary. Clerks, of course, had better promotion prospects. He found out the difference in pay after his job as a clerk at Boat of Garten came to an end at the beginning of the winter season and he was later re-employed in a junior porter's job at Fort George. With traffic increasing again in April he resumed his clerk's job again. The pattern was repeated at the end of the 1928 season as the details of his career in the table below show. In his early years on the railway Bert was keen to work at stations close to Grantown-on-Spey, where his widowed mother now lived, and managed this, apart from his postings to Fort George and Kinloss. The posts he held in his railway career of almost half a century were:

4 April	1927	Junior Clerk	Boat of Garten
2 January	1928	Junior Porter	Fort George
27 January	1928	Junior Porter	Broomhill
2 April	1928	Junior Clerk	Boat of Garten
29 October	1928	Junior Porter	Broomhill
28 March	1929	Junior Clerk	Boat of Garten
28 October	1929	Junior Clerk	Kinloss
31 March	1930	Clerk	Grantown-on-Spey
29 February	1932	Clerk	Aviemore
14 June	1940	Clerk	Invergordon
		(Relief Clerk from 1944)	
6 September	1946	Stationmaster	Achnasheen
21 November	1949	Stationmaster	Newtonmore
21 April	1952	Relief Stationmaster	Inverness
3 October	1952	Stationmaster	Newtonmore
20 April	1953	District Inspector	Inverness
3 August	1953	Stationmaster	Newtonmore
5 March	1956	District Inspector	Aviemore
5 December	1960	Stationmaster	Aviemore
13 September	1965	Chief Traffic Inspector	Inverness
5 June	1967	Terminals and Operating Assistant	Inverness
11 October	1973	Assistant Area Manager	Inverness
31 May	1975	Retired	

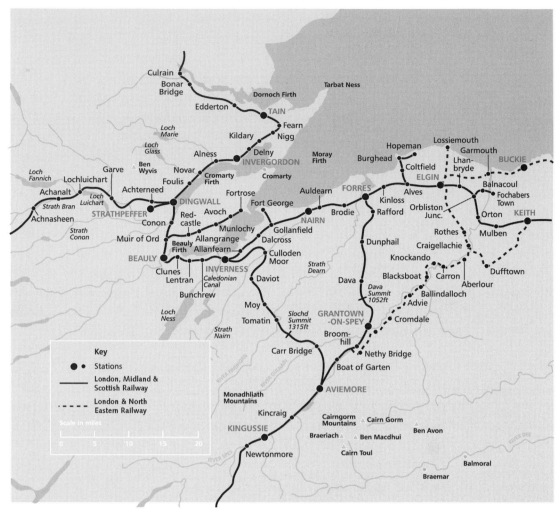

Map showing the stations where Bert Campbell had permanent appointments.

Boat of Garten, Bert Campbell's first station, had three clerks; one for passenger duties, one for goods and one for goods traffic exchanged with the London & North Eastern Railway. This was because it was the junction between the LMS line from Aviemore to Forres and the LNER's line from Craigellachie. The station was purely an LMS one, but that company's staff had to use LNER systems when dealing with the Speyside traffic. There were two ticket dating presses, two cash floats and two sets of telegraph instruments for the different lines. The cash for each company's bookings was separately accounted for and sent by train to banks in different towns. Separate returns had to be made for passenger and goods to the two companies' local and area offices. Bert recalls that the LNER Northern Scottish Area (former Great North of Scotland Railway) offices in Aberdeen were greater sticklers in seeing that the exact details of regulations were kept to than their LMS counterparts in Inverness.

The exchange of goods traffic was particularly complex. The numbers of the wagons exchanged between the companies were taken by the goods foreman and given to Bert when he was the clerk allocated to deal with the exchange. He then had to send the

Bert Campbell in 1965 while stationmaster at Aviemore.

returns not only to the companies, but also to the Railway Clearing House (RCH) for the apportionment of the carriage charges. A copy was made of the RCH return by wetting a sheet of tissue paper in a bound volume and forcing the document against it by a screw press. An RCH inspector would occasionally come up to check that the return they had received matched with the copy book.

Bert Campbell's appointments as a permanent clerk at Grantown in 1930 and then at Aviemore in 1932 involved him in the routine duties of what were nevertheless two busy stations. He was at Aviemore when war broke out and was on duty in March 1940 when there was a serious accident two miles north of the station, as related in the next chapter.

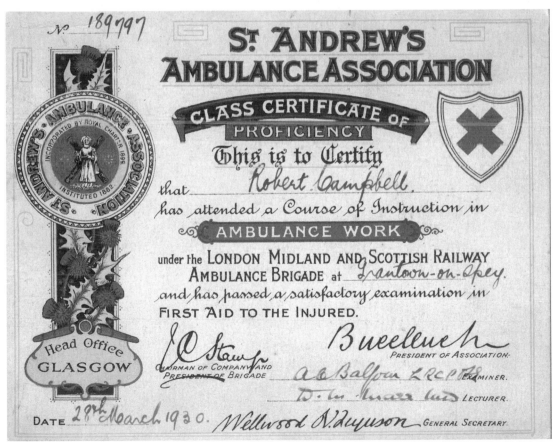

St Andrew's Ambulance Association certificate of proficiency in first aid, awarded to Bert Campbell after he had attended classes at the LMS Ambulance Brigade's Grantown-on-Spey class. The LMS encouraged their staff to undertake first aid training.

The posting at Invergordon in June 1940, Bert's first move north of Inverness, was to prove the most hectic of his railway life. Invergordon was the base for the transhipment of troops to the Shetland and Faroe Islands and each week trains with thousands of personnel would arrive at the station.

Invergordon station, where Bert Campbell spent a hectic period during World War Two. The empty station platforms shown here would have been full of service personnel when a train arrived or departed. The goods wagons arriving were frequently too many to be put in the sidings and had to be stored in one side of the loop in the station and shunted to the other when a train was due to arrive.

There were also many naval and RAF servicemen stationed in the area. On Saturdays those on monthly weekend leave would be wanting to buy tickets for the train into Inverness, while others on home leave would be wishing to book to more distant locations. Bert was sometimes faced with the situation of having to deal with a queue of 70 to 80 people for tickets while still having to operate the tablets for the signalling equipment in the booking office. For some duties, such as sending out the vast number of parcels, it became impossible to complete the specified paperwork without clogging up the whole station.

During the war Bert often worked daily shifts from 8am to 8pm at Invergordon. After the end of the war, now a married man, he acted a relief clerk in the area and then in 1946 he was appointed to his first stationmaster's position at Achnasheen on the line to Kyle of Lochalsh.

Stationmaster to Assistant Area Manager
Achnasheen was roughly halfway between Inverness and Kyle and was the station where the eastbound and westbound mid-morning and late afternoon departures from the two terminals crossed. The restaurant car on the morning departure from Inverness was

transferred to the train from Kyle at Achnasheen. The crossings of the trains which arrived at Achnasheen about lunchtime and early evening were particularly busy times of the day. While the trains were stopped, delays of up to 10 minutes might occur because some of the passengers might wish to visit the bar in the hotel on the station platform, having told the guard they would buy him a drink too.

Achnasheen station in Highland Railway days. Dert Campbell and his family lived in the station house on the first floor of the station building on the left. On the right is the Station Hotel, which was owned by the Railway, but always let out for others to manage.

Achnasheen station looking south in the 1930s with luggage waiting to be loaded on the train for Inverness. Vans for fish can be seen in the sidings in the centre background.

Achnasheen was also a busy station because it was the railhead for a significant area of Wester Ross. A bus, which connected with the trains, took passengers and mail to Gairloch. The Post Office staff transferred the mail from the train to the locked compartment of the bus. A Royal Navy lorry from the base at Aultbea also came to collect naval supplies. The four cases of bottles of beer delivered every week for the hotel at the station, along with its other supplies, required no further transport.

There was a significant amount of outward goods traffic, including sheep. Bert Campbell remembers that the sheep from the west were 'devils' to keep in the livestock pens and used to jump out of them. Fish, particularly whitefish and herring, came by lorry from the west coast and as many as three vans of fish might be added to the train to Inverness. This could delay trains but, as Bert recalls, 'they never worried about time in the West'.

The bus for Gairloch being loaded with luggage and mail at Achnasheen in the 1960s.

Visitors would also send wicker baskets containing fish they had caught in local rivers to their friends in the south. The train left Achnasheen about 7.15pm and the fish would be delivered to addresses in Edinburgh by 11.00am the next day.

Venison from deer shot on local estates was more seasonal traffic from the station. One of the bonuses of being stationmaster at Achnasheen was the haunches of venison that were sometimes sent to him from these estates.

The staff at Achnasheen consisted of the stationmaster, a clerk called Mairi Cameron, who was the daughter of the stationmaster at Strome Ferry and stayed in the hotel during the week, a porter/signalman and two signalmen. The stationmaster's house, on the first floor of the main station buildings, was a good one.

Achnasheen was a remote posting for a stationmaster. There were no shops, although there was a free pass to Dingwall for the stationmaster's wife. The village school only had two pupils, including Bert Campbell's daughter Sylvia, and church services were taken in the schoolroom once a month by the minister from Lochluichart (who would enquire after any of the congregation not present).

In spite of the distance from any centre of population, Bert recalls his period as stationmaster at Achnasheen as probably the happiest appointment in his railway career. He felt that the people in the west were generally very cheerful and friendly.

In 1949 Bert Campbell moved to become stationmaster at Newtonmore on the Perth to Inverness line. Three years later, however, he renewed his connection with the line to the west when he acted for a few weeks as relief stationmaster at Plockton, the second station east of Kyle of Lochalsh. Here he again found friendliness from the local people, and also respect for the position of stationmaster – even from the group of local tinkers who had a hut near the station.

Several months in both 1952 and 1953 were spent away from Newtonmore acting as relief stationmaster at different stations and then as a district inspector in Inverness. This was a continuation of the HR tradition of staff moving to other posts during the summer. The district inspector was responsible for the signalmen and guards and conducted annual tests to check that the staff were still up to scratch on railway rules and regulations.

In 1956 Bert Campbell left Newtonmore for Aviemore where he was based in the permanent post of district inspector. The duties included visiting the Moray Firth goods

Former Highland Railway 0–4–4 T 55053, the Dornoch branch engine, at Mound. It is preparing to attach the former Pullman restaurant car to the rear of the morning train from Wick in July 1950. It had come north on the train from Inverness. Bert Campbell served as relief stationmaster here in 1953, the year this photograph was taken. He recalls that the restaurant car staff were keen backers of horses and phoned in their bets from the Mound.

only terminal at Burghead once a week. This was to check on the state of stored wagons on the extension of the line to Hopeman which had closed in December 1957.

Bert Campbell returned to the station house he had been brought up in when he was appointed stationmaster at Aviemore in 1960. This was a time of change for the station as diesel locomotives were being introduced and the Speyside diesel railbus now ran through to Aviemore. The through coaches for Inverness via the Forres route ceased to run in 1964, by which time both it and the Speyside route trains were under threat from the Beeching report. These services were withdrawn in October 1965, just after Bert had left Aviemore for a new post in Inverness.

Bert Campbell was to be the last stationmaster at Aviemore, as the post was replaced by that of an area manager who was responsible for several stations; during the next 10 years the number of stations supervised became greater and greater while the number of station staff fell dramatically.

In Inverness Bert became first chief traffic inspector and then, as the railway staff

Aviemore station looking south from the footbridge in the early 1920s. On the left is the loading bank at which the narrow gauge forestry railway built from Loch Morlich during World War One terminated. The remains of one of the narrow gauge timber bogies can just be seen and Bert Campbell recalls playing on this as a child.

Aviemore station looking south in 1956. Comparison with the 1920s photograph shows little change apart from the removal of the goods siding on the right and the recent replacement of acetylene with electric lights. Two carriages can be seen in the siding on the left. When he was stationmaster at Aviemore Bert Campbell tried to make sure there were two spare carriages at either end of the station which could be used to strengthen crowded trains. This resulted in a complaint from the Scottish Region headquarters that Aviemore was tying up too many carriages.

structure changed, terminals and operating assistant, and finally assistant area manager, Inverness, responsible for operations over the majority of the former Highland system.

After his retirement in May 1975 Bert Campbell continued his interest in the Highland Railway and was an important source of information and photographs for those researching the history of the line. With his friend, former chief permanent way inspector Willie Duncan, he continued in his mid-90s to attend the annual meeting of the Highland Railway Society in venues as far afield as the National Railway Museum in York. Sadly Bert died in April 2005, as this book, to which he contributed so much information, was about to go to press.

Bert Campbell's retirement presentation in May 1975. On either side of Bert (front, second right) are his wife, Elizabeth, and J.D. Watson, area manager for Inverness, who made the presentation.

Burdett Cottage in Kenneth Street, Inverness, in the 1900s. Donald Campbell's wife, Christina, had been a maid to Baroness Angela Burdett-Coutts and the name of the cottage marked a gift towards the cost of the building from the Baroness. It was designed by Donald Campbell's brother, Alexander, who was an architect in Shetland. The upper floor was a separate flat and in the 1900s was the home of Lachlan Hardie, who was, like Donald Campbell, an HR guard.

Bert Campbell in 2004 outside his home Burdett Cottage, which was built by his grandparents.

CHAPTER 8

The Aviemore Loco Men and Women
The Gaults, Willie Wilkie and Jock Hay

Aviemore was one of the Highland communities that owed its existence to the railway. After the opening of Aviemore station on the Perth to Inverness line in 1863, a handful of houses, primarily for railway staff, a post office and a general store were built. The major development came, however, after 1898 when Aviemore became the junction between the new direct line to Inverness and the old line via Forres. The station was rebuilt, an engine shed opened and houses were built for the many additional railway workers as well as hotels and villas for families coming on holiday by train.

The shed's main purpose was to house and service locomotives that worked trains over the old line via Forres. Also based there were the engines which piloted trains up to Slochd and Dava summits and the station pilot.

Aviemore locomotive shed, about the time it was opened in 1898, with 4–4–0s 122 *Loch Moy* and 128 *Loch Luichart*. The man with the bowler hat who is standing to the right of 128 is probably James Smith, the locomotive foreman until 1916.

A row of houses was built by the HR in Railway Terrace, close to the engine shed, mainly for the engine crews and guards. There were also two detached houses, one for the permanent way inspector and the other for the locomotive foreman. The latter was named Ben-y-Gloe, after the initial member of the Ben class 4–4–0s introduced in 1898. The first occupant of this house was James Smith, the son of William Smith, Murdoch Paterson's engineering assistant.

The Gaults

In 1916 Willie Gault, locomotive foreman at Blair Atholl, succeeded James Smith at Aviemore when the latter was promoted to become locomotive foreman at Inverness. Willie had been born in Wick in 1871, the son of a stonemason, and had entered the service of the Highland Railway at Wick shed in the 1890s. By 1903, when he married Agnes Tait, also of Wick, he was a fitter at Blair Atholl shed and living in the station cottages there.

When he was promoted to foreman at Blair Atholl, Willie Gault was responsible for supplying engines for banking trains to Druimuachdar and others working local services to Perth. The demands on the shed's engines and crews had increased greatly after the outbreak of war in 1914 with a large number of additional trains, many carrying naval supplies and personnel to Invergordon and further north. The withdrawal of coastal shipping meant that more trains were also needed to carry domestic coal, food and other goods.

The houses for locomotive crews at Railway Terrace, Aviemore, are in the right foreground of this photograph of 1973. The detached house on the left is Ben-y-Gloe, the shed foreman's house. The permanent way inspector had a similar detached house at the other end of the terrace.

0–6–4 T 44 heading a permanent way train. This was one of the banking tanks built primarily to assist trains from Blair Atholl to Dalnaspidal. Willie Gault had five of these engines under his charge when he was locomotive foreman at Blair Atholl.

At Aviemore Willie was faced with an even greater task of ensuring there was sufficient motive power for trains working on the Forres route as well as the main line. There were also additional timber trains from the Strathspey area where trees were being felled by the Canadian Forestry Corps.

The end of World War One lessened the pressure on Willie Gault, but his position in charge of the largest engine shed on the HR outside Inverness and Perth was still a demanding one. He was responsible for all the locomotive staff, ranging from the fitters who maintained the locomotives to the crews who drove them. There were a dozen engines based at the shed, while

Willie Gault stands second from the right in front of a Loch 4–4–0 at Aviemore engine shed.

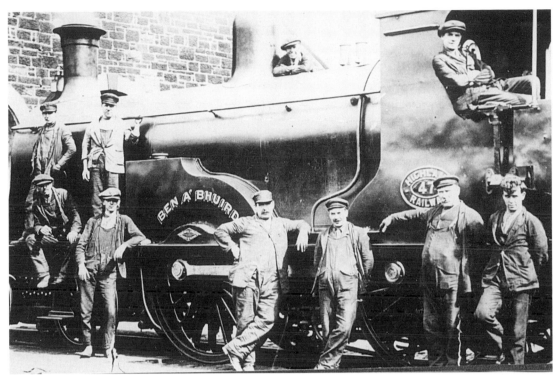

A group of loco men photographed in front of 4–4–0 *Ben A' Bhuird* at Aviemore shed in 1922. A diagram on the back identifies the men and, in some cases, gives their nicknames. Bob Gault is sitting in the cab and W. McLean ('Pimple') is behind the dome. From left to right on the engine are D. McKay, A. Rae ('Washie') and A. Kennedy ('Samson'). Standing on the ground, from the left are: J. Jack, R. Blackhall of Keith shed, C. Ross ('Nigger'), A. Munro ('Snooks') and R. Grant ('Boatie').

others needed servicing after working to Aviemore from elsewhere on the Highland Railway.

The amalgamation of the HR into the London, Midland and Scottish Railway did not affect the working of Aviemore shed greatly during Willie Gault's period as locomotive foreman. Although new LMS locomotives were introduced on the main line from the late 1920s, Aviemore's own allocation was of purely Highland locomotives until they began to be replaced by former Caledonian Railway locomotives in 1939.

Willie Gault had five sons and twin daughters. Agnes, his wife, died after the birth of the twins and his sister came down from Wick to look after the family at Ben-y-Gloe. After retirement Willie went to live with his son Hugh at Ben View, Aviemore, until his death in 1958. He had built this house and the adjacent cottage, Craig View, out of

Ben View (at rear), together with the adjacent Craig View, was built from railway sleepers by Willie Gault. There were several of these sleeper houses in the Strathspey and Badenoch area. Sleepers were one of the less expensive building materials and railwaymen such as Willie Gault were both given priority in purchasing them and paid a reduced rate.

railway sleepers. Willie was a skilled woodworker who built wheelbarrows, timber gates and bridges for farmers.

Four of Willie's five sons and both his daughters worked on the railway at some stage in their lives. The eldest son, also named Willie, was a clerk at Aviemore when John Campbell was the stationmaster. He later emigrated to New Zealand to join his brother, Angus.

Bob Gault followed his father's footsteps in eventually being in charge of engine sheds. He started his career at Aviemore, but then moved to be an apprentice at St Rollox Works in Glasgow, as this was where Willie felt his son would receive the best training in locomotive maintenance. He returned to Aviemore in 1940 before becoming the night foreman at Inverness shed. In British Railways days Bob Gault became shedmaster at Forres and then moved on to similar positions at Kittybrewster (Aberdeen), Hawick and finally Dunfermline, from where he retired.

Bob's brother, Alexander, started his working life as a baker, but then also went to St Rollox for training as a fitter's mate. He joined the maintenance staff at Inverness shed for the remainder of his railway career. Another brother, Hugh Gault, remained at Aviemore shed, progressing from cleaner to fireman and then to driver. The younger Gault children, Bunty and Elma, worked as cleaners at the shed during World War Two.

Bob Gault (back row, second left) when he was shedmaster at Forres in the 1950s. The photograph shows the Forres railway ambulance class. Sitting in the centre of the front row is a Dr Brewster, who helped to instruct the class. On the left of the front row is A.C. Jeffreys, district locomotive superintendent at Inverness, while on the right is Tom Ross ('Darkest Africa') who coaled the engine at Forres shed.

The tradition of working on the railways has been continued into the 21st century by a further two generations of the Gault family. Three of Willie Gault's grandsons, Willie, Callum and Billy, have worked at Inverness depot where his great-grandson, Norman, is also now based.

Wartime

The outbreak of World War Two in 1939 meant that the demands on Aviemore shed once again increased massively, with troop and supply trains constantly passing through. New sidings were built at the north end of the station to cope with the additional traffic, particularly the timber that was being felled in the area by the Newfoundland lumberjacks and Canadian Forestry Corps. LMS 2–8–0s from Grangemouth worked the timber trains south to the Forth port. A hostel with 32 beds for train crews working traffic from Grangemouth and Perth was built in 1943. It provided better sleeping accommodation than was possible in the dormitory coaches that had previously been used.

The Gaults: first generation. Willie Gault, shed foreman, (third from right on ground), stands in front of 2–4–0 35A *Isla Bank* at Aviemore in about 1922. The engine was one of the last HR 2–4–0s in service. The other people in the photograph are drivers, firemen or shed staff.

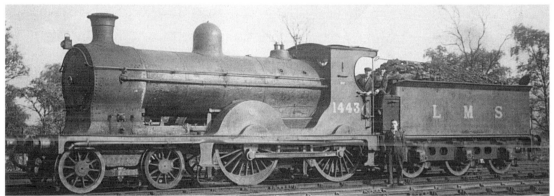

The Gaults: second generation. Willie's son, Hugh Gault (right on footplate), was the fireman on former Caledonian Railway 4–4–0 14436 at Aviemore in the 1940s. The driver (left on footplate) was William Fraser.

The Gaults: third and fourth generations. Hugh's son Callum Gault, shift supervisor at Inverness depot, is on the right, and Callum's son Norman, a shunter at the depot, is beside 08788 in this 2004 photograph.

Aviemore, looking towards the station, June 1956. On the left is the entrance to the locomotive yard; in the centre behind the double armed signal are the sidings laid during World War Two and on the far right, behind Aviemore North signal cabin, the roof of Ben View can just be made out.

In March 1940 there was a serious accident which resulted in the death of a locomotive crew, an event that is still remembered today by those who worked at Aviemore shed. The drawbar coupling on a northbound coal train broke as it entered the loop at Slochd summit and the guards van and 21 wagons started to run back towards Aviemore. The guard, George Moyes, realising his handbrake was not slowing the wagons, jumped from his van and landed without serious injury. The wagons increased speed as they rushed back through Carr Bridge station.

James Calder, the signalman at Carr Bridge, contacted Aviemore signal cabin and station to halt the following double-headed freight train, but it had just set out for the north. Bert Campbell, who was in the Aviemore booking office, used the railway phone link to alert Chrissie Lobban, the crossing keeper at Dalfaber crossing. She rushed out with a handlamp showing red, but this was not seen by the train crews. About two miles north of Aviemore the train was struck by the runaway wagons.

The pilot engine of the freight train, 4–4–0 14381 *Loch Ericht* took the full force of the collision and the Aviemore driver, Willie Perry, and fireman Sandy Malcolm were killed instantly. The locomotive ended up lying on its side at right angles to the track, buried under a pile of demolished wagons. The train engine, a Black Five 4–6–0, was

4–4–0 14381 *Loch Ericht* piloting a Jones Goods 4–6–0 on a northbound goods train at Slochd summit in 1929. Eleven years later the locomotive was destroyed when it was piloting a northbound goods train from Aviemore and was hit by wagons which had broken away from the previous goods train at Slochd.

Carr Bridge station in 1931, looking north. The wagons which broke away from the goods train at Slochd ran down the gradient through the station until they hit the following train. After the accident in 1940 the LMS installed a set of trap points and a sand drag at the north end of this station so that any further runaways could be derailed here.

little damaged and the crew relatively unscathed, although the guard, Duncan Mackintosh, received facial injuries. Roland Bond, the LMS mechanical engineer for Scotland, recalled that the mangled remains of *Loch Ericht* were cut up on the spot as it was so badly damaged.

There was much sympathy among the close-knit railway community in Aviemore for the families of the crew who had been killed. Sandy Malcolm's widow was found employment by the LMS, first as a cleaner at Aviemore shed, then on the staff of the Aviemore train crew hostel and finally as matron supervising another new wartime hostel at Inverness.

Mrs Malcolm was only one of a number of women employed on the railway at Aviemore during World War Two; previously they had only worked as clerks in the station. In addition to the staff of the train crew's hostel, there were four engine cleaners, including Bunty and Elma Gault, and four women guards. The cleaning and guards jobs again became the preserve of men at the end of the war.

Three former Highland Railway locomotives – LMS 14398 *Ben Alder*, 4–4–0 14379 *Loch Insh* and 4–6–0 14690 *Dalcross Castle*. The photograph was taken from the entrance to Aviemore shed in 1946. Three years later there were no Highland locomotives left at Aviemore.

Willie Wilkie and Jock Hay

The wartime traffic meant that there were more vacancies for engine crews, especially at sheds like Aviemore which now had extra duties. This led to far quicker promotion for engine cleaners, the first stage on the ladder to becoming a driver, than would have been possible previously. In the 1930s progress from being a cleaner depended on a fireman moving up to be a passed fireman (who could also drive locomotives when necessary) and eventually taking the place of a driver who had retired or died. Promotion was purely on the basis of seniority.

Two of the staff who joined the LMS in 1940 – Willie Wilkie and Jock Hay – moved quickly up from cleaner to fireman. Willie Wilkie from Nethy Bridge had worked as message boy in the village and then as a farmhand at Dell of Rothiemurchus before becoming a cleaner at Aviemore.

Jock Hay started his railway career at Forres shed. He had been working as a charge hand in a grain mill in Forres when he learned from the crew of the goods loco, which was shunting coal for the mill into its siding, that there were vacancies for locomotive cleaners. Jock wasted no time in applying.

When he was on night shift as a cleaner at Forres, Jock also had to 'knock up' the crews for the early turn from the shed. He recalled that when he got no response from one house at 4am he battered the door 'like the Gestapo' to rouse the driver. Unfortunately it was the wrong house and an irate housewife sent him away with some choice words.

One of Jock's first jobs a year after he had gained promotion to a fireman at Aviemore in 1941 was on Barney 0–6–0 17699 which left Aviemore with material for the new Dalanraoch signal cabin. This replaced the previous signal box half a mile to the north as part of the measures to increase the capacity of the line for wartime traffic. Willie Duncan was involved in this project on the permanent way side. The job took longer than anticipated and the locomotive had to run down to Blair Atholl to take more water. The crew arrived back with it at Aviemore at midnight, 18 hours after they had set out.

Fireman Jock Hay (left) and driver Arthur Lay, with the shovel, on the footplate of Caley Benny 4 4–0 14463 in 1949. These locomotives were known to the Highland crews as Caley Bennies because they were inside cylinder 4–4–0s like the Highland Ben locomotives they often replaced.

Willie Wilkie also had a memorable journey during wartime. He fired the locomotive with a train of mines as far as Helmsdale. He and his driver had been expecting to return 'on the cushions' in one of the carriages on the southbound passenger train, but when they arrived at the station they were told they had been rostered to take over the pilot engine of the double-headed train. The driver had unfortunately drunk too much at a local hostelry and was incapable of taking over the control of the locomotive. Willie therefore had to drive as well as fire the engine to Inverness and, additionally, hand over the tablets for each section of the single line. When the train stopped at stations, he closed the firebox door so that the slumped driver could not be seen.

There was also a lighter side to railway life. The staff were known to one another by nicknames; Willie Wilkie was 'Wendell' and Jock Hay was 'Jock Straw'. Practical jokes were played on colleagues. Willie Wilkie recalls arriving back from his turn of duty to find that his new bike had disappeared from the cycle shed. He searched everywhere for it and then found it hanging from the rafters of the locomotive shed, from where he retrieved it by standing on top of the coal on an engine's tender. He later found out who was responsible, but said nothing when asked by the culprit to collect a dozen fresh eggs for him from one of the cottages at Slochd when he was on pilot duties. Willie extracted his revenge by boiling them hard in a bucket of hot water from the engine's boiler before handing them over!

Caley Benny 4–4–0 54455 piloting a Black Five 4–6–0 out of Aviemore on a train for Inverness in about 1950. The 4–4–0, which was based at Aviemore shed, would probably come off at Slochd summit. These were the two most common types of locomotives that Jock Hay and Willie Wilkie worked over the Highland main line.

Nationalisation of the railways brought some change, in that from the 1950s the Speyside line locomotives from the former London and North Eastern Railway Boat of Garten shed now ran to Aviemore shed. Here the tenders could be filled more easily with coal from the coaling stage than from wagons at Boat of Garten. The goods trains from Keith, which carried whisky from the local distilleries to bonded warehouses in the south, were also extended from Boat of Garten to Aviemore.

The loco men disperse

In the mid-1950s the railway was still the largest employer in Aviemore. 130 people, out of a total population of 650, worked on the railway and about 80 of these worked at the engine shed.

Former Great North of Scotland Railway 4–4–0 62256 heads a train loaded with whisky barrels from the Speyside distilleries into Boat of Garten in 1950. There were occasions when whisky was pilfered from the barrels. Holes were bored through the wagon floor into the barrel and an amount of whisky drained off. A small wooden bung, covered with brown boot polish to disguise the new wood, was then put in the hole.

The shed even fielded its own team – Loco Rangers – in the local football league. Major changes were, however, about to happen.

In 1958 a diesel railbus was introduced on the Speyside line and the service from Craigellachie to Boat of Garten was extended to run from Elgin to Aviemore. The engine shed at 'the Boat' was closed and Aviemore crews worked both passenger and goods trains on the Speyside route. The introduction of diesel locomotives on all services on the Highland main line soon followed and by April 1962 steam had vanished from Aviemore shed.

A Park Royal railbus pauses at Boat of Garten on an Elgin-Aviemore working, not long before the withdrawal of the service in 1965. The railbuses were the earliest diesels to be introduced in the Highlands. When the first railbus was put on show at Aviemore in 1958 no fewer than 315 people, almost half the village's population, queued to see it. The railbuses were known as 'sputniks' after the contemporary pioneering Russian space satellites.

With most of the maintenance of the diesel locomotives being carried out at Inverness and certain duties, such as the railbus and the station pilot, now being crewed by one man, the number of staff in the engine shed was halved. Worse, however, was to follow, as the Beeching Report led in 1965 to the closure of the Forres route and the withdrawal of passenger services on the Speyside route as well as the local trains to Inverness.

The end of these services meant the closure of the locomotive shed. Apart from John Jack and Jimmy Gray, who worked the Speyside goods service until it too was withdrawn in 1968, all the men at Aviemore depot were either made redundant or had to move to railway jobs away from the village.

This was a major problem for drivers such as Willie Wilkie who wished to retain their home at Aviemore. He now lived in a house in the village after moving from a cottage built for a signalman at the former Dalraddy crossing two miles south of Aviemore. The result of his transfer to Inverness in 1965 meant that he had to rise at 3am to catch the 4.10am train to Inverness to take up his driving turn and he only returned late in the evening. He left the railway, but later rejoined it as a guard, living away from home during the week at Wick.

Other drivers also found the travelling to and from Inverness difficult. Hugh Gault changed jobs and became a relief porter based at Newtonmore. Other drivers, such as Jock Hay, moved their homes away from Aviemore. After being based at Perth depot Jock transferred in 1968 to Inverness. He retired in 1987 after spending his final years on the railway instructing new drivers.

Following its closure, the track to and inside Aviemore shed was lifted and the building let out to local firms. In 1975, however, it was acquired by the Strathspey Railway, who were about to reopen the line to Boat of Garten for steam trains. Track was relaid into the shed yard and rails from the former HR locomotive depot at Perth laid inside the building. Among the locomotives housed there today are LMS 4–6–0 5025 and Caledonian Railway 0–6–0 828, both members of classes which were once based at the shed and driven by Willie Wilkie and Jock Hay.

Aviemore locomotive shed in 2003, with the Strathspey Railway's 2–6–0 46512 outside. The shed has changed little since its opening in 1898. Alone among all the former Scottish engine sheds, it still houses steam locomotives.

Today the economy of Aviemore is based on tourism and many new buildings have been erected between the 1960s and the 2000s. Happily not only the engine shed, but also the station (restored in 1998) and the HR houses have survived as a reminder of Aviemore's railway origins.

CHAPTER 9

The Railway and Railway Staff in Inverness
Alexander MacDonald: A Head Office Official; Lachy Russell, Willie Peddie and the Gaults: Lochgorm Works Staff

On 22 May 1890 *The Scottish Highlander* newspaper carried an article entitled 'Inverness and the Highland Railway'. In it 'AM' wrote how the population of the town had risen from 12,793 in 1851 to almost 20,000 in 1890. During the same period the value of the property in Inverness had increased from £23,603 to almost £90,000. The buildings in the town now occupied three times the built up area in 1855 and the 'class of houses now is not to be compared with the class of houses then'. The writer of the article stated that:

> These figures indicate a great advance in the material prosperity of the burgh, and it is felt to be very largely due to the Highland Railway Company, and especially to the presence of its head offices and works in Inverness. At present there are nearly 900 people employed in the town in connection with the Highland Railway, and of these about 800 are artisans. The amount paid in wages and salaries each year is over £60,000, and of this sum it is calculated that over £50,000 or about £1,000 a week goes to the artisan classes. The railway works are the chief, practically only, industry in Inverness.

Inverness on a Highland Railway postcard published in 1902. Many of the buildings, including the cathedral in the right centre shown here, had been built after the coming of the railway. To the left of the cathedral are houses built on ground which Sir Alexander Matheson, the HR chairman, had purchased for development. The street names reflected Matheson connections. Ardross Street, for instance, was named after one of Sir Alexander's estates.

Station Square, showing the station on the left and the Station Hotel on the right. The Station Hotel was built in 1856, but was run by tenants until 1878. The building was extended several times. It became the premier hotel in Inverness and was probably one of the HR's most profitable ventures. The 1901 census shows that in addition to Herbert Wolf, the hotel manager, the other staff included a housekeeper, clerks, barmaids, still room maids, cook, linen maids, cellar men and bakers.

The railway was of great significance as the major employer in the town. It also created employment for others. The HR used local architects and lawyers and placed orders with Inverness firms while railway families patronised local shops and tradesfolk in Inverness. It was also of importance because it was the terminus of lines from the north, south, east and west; this placed the town at the centre of the Highland Railway system. Without doubt the railway reinforced the role of Inverness as 'the capital of the Highlands'.

The impact of the railway

The coming of the railway provided a quicker and cheaper form of transport than had been available by road, in spite of the improvements carried out by the Commission for Roads and Bridges in the Highlands. The cost of transporting barley from Badenoch to Inverness was almost the same as bringing it by sea from the Baltic. The fares charged by the mail coach from Perth to Inverness, which took around 12 hours, restricted the number of people who could travel to and from the town.

Shipping by sea or through the Caledonian Canal provided an alternative form of transport to Inverness before the railway. This was especially the case for goods, such as cattle and coal, which came up the east coast, but there was also a weekly passenger service from Leith and, in the summer, a daily passenger service from Glasgow via the Caledonian Canal.

When the link to the south was completed the railway captured almost all the long-distance traffic from the roads and the majority of traffic which had previously come by water transport. There were exceptions: in the 1900s twice as much coal still came by sea as by rail. The Caledonian Canal steamers to Banavie, near Fort William, also continued to run until World War Two, although they were often used by tourists in conjunction with railway journeys.

The railway had an impact on the lives of Inverness people. In her book *Inverness Before Railways*, published in 1885, Isabel Harriet Anderson wrote:

> *Since the opening of the railway in 1855, not only have a number of strangers come to reside in the Highland Capital, causing a spirit of competition to arise, and an impetus to be given to progress and activity, but their ever-extending arrival and settlement have caused a gradual, but complete revolution in the ways of what had for many years been a quiet and exclusive little town in which the advent of a stranger from the South was an event apt to be regarded with a degree of trepidation as well as excitement.*

The railway changed the townscape of Inverness. The building of the station in Academy Street led to much development in the area. In the early 1860s a group of local businessmen, headed by Charles Fraser Mackintosh, a lawyer and future MP, bought up property between Academy and Church Streets and developed Union Street as one of the

Queensgate, Inverness, in the 1910s; the post office is the imposing building on the centre right. The street was laid out in 1884, as the commercial and business life of the town was increasingly concentrated near the station. The offices of the Midland Railway are on the left. The East Coast Railways (North Eastern and Great Northern), and the West Coast (Caledonian and London and North Western) and North British Railways also had offices near the station. Their purpose was to ensure traffic beyond Perth and also the English Border went by their routes.

Aerial view of Inverness in the late 1930s. The passenger station is in the middle left and the goods yard is in the right foreground. From the passenger station lines lead across the picture in front of Lochgorm Works to the south and east. The line to the north curves round from the passenger station towards the River Ness.

town's main commercial thoroughfares. In addition to the railway company's own offices and the Station Hotel, other hotels, shops and offices were established near the station.

The opening of the goods station had a similarly significant effect on the Eastgate area, where a large number of warehouses were built, particularly to hold dry goods and groceries for wholesalers who moved from the quayside where they had previously been supplied by sea. The harbour, however, continued to house the coal merchants and the coal coming by rail was also dealt with there. The two Inverness livestock markets were either located (MacDonald Fraser) or relocated (Hamilton) adjacent to the goods yard at Eastgate, so that the cattle and sheep being sold could be easily transported by railway.

The Falcon Foundry was also established close to the railway so that its products could be moved by rail. The Highland Railway was also a customer of the foundry, which, among other orders, supplied the ironwork that covers the end of platforms 1 and 2 at Inverness station. The foundry closed in the early 1880s; one reason was probably competition from the Northern Agricultural and Implement Foundry, which also lay close to the railway; the chairman of this was Cluny Macpherson who was an HR director. In 1895 the Northern Agricultural Foundry amalgamated with other foundries and ironworks to become the Rose Street Foundry. It received many orders from the HR because the company did not have its own foundry facilities. As it expanded the Rose Street Foundry joined Lochgorm Works as the only significant industries in Inverness.

William Forbes, the stationmaster, wearing the top hat, as all holders of his office did at Inverness in HR days, inside Inverness station in the 1880s or 1890s. He was moved to Inverness from Grantown-on-Spey and retired in 1898. He is standing in the original section of Inverness station. Through the wall can be seen the ironwork over platforms 1 and 2 which was made in 1878 by the Falcon Foundry that lay close to the station.

Inverness station in 1957. The original Inverness and Nairn Railway station was the second roof bay from the right. The bay on the far right was built for the Inverness and Ross-shire Railway trains and the two on the left were added in 1878.

The trial erection of an HR footbridge at Rose Street Foundry for Buchrew station in June 1913. As well as footbridges, chairs for rails, points, crossings, gates and many other castings were made for the railway. Although the manufacture of chairs ceased in 1929, it continued to supply the LMS with mileposts. As Resistance Welders, the company still maintained its connection with railways in 1956 by supplying flash-butt welding machines for long welded rails to London Transport and British Railways.

The jobs that the railway brought to the town, directly or indirectly, led to an expansion of housing in Inverness. Because of the availability of housing in Inverness the Highland Railway found no need to build accommodation for its staff. One exception was Railway Terrace, close to Inverness station, which was constructed in 1889 for the crew of the breakdown crane, so that they would be immediately available if an accident occurred.

Many of the operating and station staff lived relatively close to the railway. The 1901 census shows, for example, that there were two porters, two engine drivers, two engine fitters, two engine cleaners, a railway cleaner and a railway clerk living in Victoria Square. Some were lodgers who were staying in the houses of other railway workers.

In the 1900s the houses lived in by the different grades of staff reflected their income. The porters, engine drivers and workers from

Ardconnel Terrace in 2004. Several railway workers lived in this street, particularly in Tulloch Buildings (with balconies and pillars). In 1901 the HR employees in Ardconnel Terrace included two clerks, a ticket inspector, a vacuum brake fitter and an engine cleaner.

Lochgorm often lived in the tenements near the centre of Inverness. The Highland Railway's senior officers mainly lived in the villas towards what was then the edge of the built-up area of the town. Thomas Wilson, the HR's general manager, lived even further out at Riverdale, a large house in its own grounds, on Island Bank Road.

The erecting shop at Lochgorm Works, probably in the 1890s. As well as overhauling locomotives Lochgorm built engines until 1906.

Head office and Lochgorm Works Staff

The number of railway staff employed by the Highland Railway and the further employment that they and their families created was of the greatest importance to Inverness. The article in *The Scottish Highlander* in May 1890 stated that if the HR was taken over by one of southern Scottish companies Lochgorm Works would be closed and: 'It would reduce our population at one stroke by at least a fifth and it would leave a large number of houses and shops which are now occupied in the burgh and which pay rates and taxes unoccupied.'

Although *The Scottish Highlander* article concentrated on the jobs that would be lost at Lochgorm Works, the loss of head office posts would have posed another serious threat. They were fewer in number, but they included a number of well-paid professional jobs, such as railway administrators, accountants and locomotive and civil engineers. The other railway posts – station and operating and track staff – would have been less likely to be affected, as would the Station Hotel staff.

In 1906 a threat to railway jobs in Inverness emerged when the Highland Railway proposed amalgamation, not with a southern company, but with the Great North of Scotland Railway. The headquarters of the amalgamated line would have been in Aberdeen, with a resulting loss of head office posts in Inverness.

There was also much concern about Lochgorm Works as the GNSR had built new workshops in Inverurie in 1901. The Highland directors stated that Lochgorm would be maintained for repairs and indeed be developed, but there was much hostility to the proposals. In the event, although there was a large majority of HR shareholders voting in favour of the amalgamation, the scheme was dropped because 42 percent had not voted.

There was no such reprieve for railway posts in Inverness, however, when the London, Midland and Scottish Railway was formed in 1923. Many of the head office posts were transferred south and the senior posts that remained there – the district traffic superintendent and the district civil engineer – were responsible first to the Scottish headquarters in Glasgow and ultimately to the LMS headquarters in London. There was also a significant loss of jobs at Lochgorm Works which was spread out over a longer period in the 1920s.

Lochgorm Works from the entrance foot bridge in the 1900s (left) and the late 1950s (right). The two boilers from withdrawn locomotives in the earlier photograph supplied steam which powered the shafting machinery in the works. In the 1900s the workshops were still a significant source of employment in Inverness, but their importance declined after the LMS transferred work away in the 1920s.

From the 1920s there was increasing competition from motorised road transport for both passengers and goods. The railway companies reacted to the threat to local passenger travel by taking a financial interest in bus operators. In 1930 the LMS merged its Highland bus interests into the new Inverness-based Highland Transport Company, which was chaired by Provost Sir Alexander MacEwen.

From the 1950s the importance of the railways to Inverness declined as road and air competition increased. Its role as a major employer also declined. Lochgorm Works closed in 1959 and many more jobs were lost when diesel locomotives were introduced, train services were cut back and the administrative work at the Inverness offices reduced. In 2005 the importance of the railway to Inverness, now a city of 60,000 people, has declined from half a century ago. Nevertheless it is still important to the economy of the city, particularly as far as tourism is concerned, and the diesel depot is still a significant centre of engineering skills.

The train departure board at Inverness on 8 October 1965. Some plates had been blanked out after the services, such as the local trains to Tain, had been withdrawn. The Aviemore local services had been withdrawn five months earlier and the trains via Grantown-on-Spey ceased from 18 October 1965.

Alexander MacDonald

The railway staff played a significant part in the life of the community in Inverness and were members of organisations such as the Field Club and the Gaelic Society. There were also several railway employees who were town councillors and baillies (magistrates elected from among the councillors). The baillies included H.H. Ward, the HR's hotels manager, and John Mackay, who retired from the LMS as a signalman in Millburn box in 1935.

One head office official who was involved in the cultural and civic life of Inverness was Alexander MacDonald. The County of Inverness volume of *The Third Statistical Account of Scotland*, published in 1985, picked him out as one of the notable people identified with the town.

Alexander MacDonald's life is also a reminder of the opportunities the railway could provide for the able young men in the Highlands whose parents did not have the resources to send them to university. He was born a crofter's son in Glenmoriston, near Loch Ness, in 1860 and, in probably his second job, became a clerk in the HR accountant's office in 1879. He was appointed chief auditor and accountant of the Highland Railway at the age of 43 in 1904.

The author Mairi MacDonald, Alexander's daughter, wrote a novel, *Highland Coronach*, which has as its central character a crofter's son who had an identical career to her father's. Some parts of the book are clearly fiction, but others draw on Alexander MacDonald's life. This

Letter from Peter Drummond, the HR's locomotive superintendent, to Alexander MacDonald, recently appointed chief accountant. Other surviving letters between chief officers sometimes have a similarly sharp tone.

would appear to be the case when she writes of her character feeling that the planned amalgamation with the LMS would mean that the Inverness offices would be of small importance. He thought of:

> *Those great rooms silent; the long stone stairway no longer ringing under the tread of hurrying feet; the imposing boardroom no longer to be the scene of these dignified monthly meetings of directors. It seemed as if a warm sheltering friendship were slipping out of his life.*
>
> *He found himself facing a crossroads... An important post awaited him in London. Should he accept? He was now sixty-three...*

The Highland Railway head offices on the west side of Station Square, Inverness, which were opened in 1876 and designed by the Inverness architecture firm of Matthews and Lawrie. Now known as Highland Rail House, they are no longer used by railway staff, but have a variety of tenants, including the offices of the local Member of the Scottish Parliament.

It seems highly likely that Alexander MacDonald was also offered a post at the LMS headquarters, as he had made improvements in railway accounting methods. If so, he, like his fictional counterpart, turned it down and retired after a year's service with the new company.

Alexander would have been loath to leave the Highlands as he was also a leading Gaelic scholar and author and was an authority on Gaelic poetry and tradition and also on Highland bagpipe music. Known as 'Gleannach' in Gaelic circles he joined the Gaelic Society of Inverness in 1881 and became one of its honorary chieftains. He contributed papers to both the Gaelic Society and the Inverness Field Club.

Alexander MacDonald became a member of the town council in 1924 after he was asked to stand for election so that the community could benefit from his financial skills. The hero of his daughter's novel also followed this road, but died of a heart attack in the council chamber during a heated debate about railway and bus services on Sundays. This section appears to be one of the fictional passages of the book written for dramatic effect. The Inverness newspapers for February 1928 show otherwise. A motion was put forward by Baillie John Macleod opposing the running of railway excursions on Sundays. The successful rejection of the motion was proposed by Baillie Arthur Smith, the former Highland Railway architect, and seconded by Alexander MacDonald, who pointed out that no restrictions were being put forward for buses on Sundays. Alexander collapsed during the meeting and died of heart failure after being taken to his home in Southside Road by ambulance.

Glencona, the house built for Alexander MacDonald and his wife, Jessie, in Southside Road, Inverness, in the early years of the 20th century. This was one of several villas in the area which were the homes of HR chief officers. William Roberts, the chief civil engineer, lived at Rockburn and William McIntyre, assistant traffic manager at Fern Villa, both also in Southside Road, while William Gowenlock, retired secretary of the company, and William Garrow, retired superintendent of the line, lived in Muirfield Road.

The funeral of Alexander MacDonald at Tomnahurich cemetery was an appropriately Highland one and the cortège reflected the different aspects of his life. The town council members and officers and three pipers preceded the hearse and it was followed by representatives of the LMS and the Gaelic Society and 'a large number of the general public'.

Lachy Russell

The railway head office was one important source of railway employment in Inverness. Another was Lochgorm Works. On a visit to Lochgorm in 1958 I met Lachy Russell, the longest-serving of the former HR employees at the works, who told me of the changes in the fortunes of the works he had seen while working there.

Lachy had started at Lochgorm in 1912 when Peter Drummond was still locomotive superintendent and had worked under Drummond's three successors. He had particularly disliked David Urie, the last locomotive superintendent.

David Urie's period in control of Lochgorm Works had started promisingly. After Urie arrived in 1922 Lachy recalled that much new machinery was acquired. This was in spite of the fact that the Highland Railway was due to be merged into the LMS on 1 January 1923 and would not normally have committed capital expenditure on its workshops at that late stage in its existence. The minutes of the Highland Railway board show nonetheless that in September and October 1922 it was agreed to spend £2,600 on new machinery for Lochgorm.

The reason for this expenditure was probably because the HR board felt that the machinery would help to secure the future of Lochgorm as a major repair facility once the LMS was formed. If this was the case their plans completely misfired. In 1925 David Urie was appointed to the post of LMS mechanical engineer for Scotland, based at the former Caledonian Railway works at St Rollox. After taking up his new position he returned to Lochgorm to order that much of the machinery acquired in 1922 should be sent down to St Rollox. He also said that 60 men should be sacked. Lachy recalled Urie's return to Lochgorm with some bitterness; he had walked though the works without acknowledging any of the men who had been his direct responsibility.

Former Highland Railway locomotives under repair in Lochgorm Works in 1936. By this time major overhauls of Highland engines were carried out at St Rollox Works in Glasgow.

Former Caledonian Railway 4–4–0 of Wick shed, with one set of wheels removed, outside Lochgorm Works in 1958.

The reason for the loss of jobs at Lochgorm was that the LMS had larger and more modern works in Scotland and much of the heavy overhaul work on locomotives and carriages was transferred to St Rollox in Glasgow and wagon overhaul to Barassie in Ayrshire. The LMS in fact considered closing Lochgorm along with Perth, Barrow and Stoke works, but had decided 'For policy and other reasons, carriage, wagon and local [locomotive] repairs at Lochgorm works could continue.'

By 1928 there were new concerns. It was reported that when locomotive repair jobs fell vacant they were not filled and when apprentices finished their time they were dismissed and the apprenticeships not filled. The number of men working in the wagon shop fell from 65 to 20 in the five years after 1923.

In 1929 there were further job losses when it was decided by the LMS that the works should deal with 'light and service repairs only'. Carriage repairs now ceased completely and Needlefield carriage and wagon works became a carriage depot. Some light wagon repairs were carried out in two bays of Lochgorm. The works' survival was helped by the fact that Inverness engine shed had no major repair facilities and jobs which might have been carried out in similar-sized sheds were sent over to the works.

Lachy Russell survived the job cuts and continued to work at Lochgorm for as long as the works remained open. During World War Two he was involved in dealing with the increased pressure of repairs caused by the additional traffic, as he had been in 1914–18.

Lachy had sight in only one eye, but this did not stop him being a skilled fitter. In the 1950s new apprentices were allocated to work with him for their first two months after starting at Lochgorm, as it was felt he would give them a good grounding in engineering.

The apprentices: Willie Peddie and the Gaults

There were 12 apprentices when I visited Lochgorm in 1958. Among them was Willie Peddie, son of the chief permanent way inspector at Inverness (who was Willie Duncan's predecessor in this post), and cousins Callum and Billy Gault, grandsons of the former locomotive foreman at Inverness whose career is described in Chapter 8. Another cousin, Willie Gault, had completed his apprenticeship at Lochgorm a couple of years earlier.

The methods of work had not changed much since the days of the Highland Railway; measurement was still being done by callipers rather than by micrometers. The working conditions were fairly basic; no hot water was provided between March and October when the heating was turned off. In the winter chisels were put on radiators and washers in pockets to warm them up.

Former Caledonian Railway 0–6–0 T shunting the sidings at Lochgorm Works in the late 1950s with Murdo McLeod, one of the Inverness shunters, on the footplate. This and some of the other photos of Lochgorm were taken by Willie Peddie, one of the last apprentices there from 1956 to 1959. He later became mechanical and plant engineer for Railtrack Scotland and was also chairman of the Scottish Railway Preservation Society.

Every week a Black Five 4–6–0 would come in for an intermediate overhaul. The locomotives would be separated from their tenders and the wheels removed from both. Each apprentice worked with a fitter on an individual locomotive or tender for the three to four weeks they were in Lochgorm. The apprentice was given the job of cleaning out the inside of the tender tank.

Former Caledonian Railway and LMS Black Five locomotives under repair in Lochgorm Works in 1954.

As well as engines from Inverness, Black Fives would also come from Perth, Aberdeen and St Rollox sheds. Inverness locomotives were given special attention as their drivers could easily complain to the staff of the adjacent works if they were not satisfactory. Former Caledonian Railway 4–4–0s from local sheds also came into the works for attention to any defects that had arisen in service.

The apprentices in 1958 were the last to serve their time at Lochgorm. A review of British Railways workshops, influenced no doubt by the imminent dieselisation of the Highland lines, decided that it would close. There was local opposition to the decision, but to no avail. Lochgorm closed in June 1959 and 77 jobs disappeared.

Three Lochgorm fitters stand in front of Western Region 0–6–0 PT 1649. In the centre is Alan Brown and on the right is Alec 'Handful' Robertson. This engine was one of two transferred to Scotland in 1957 to work the Dornoch branch because of its light axle loading. On its arrival in the Highlands it was found it needed attention in the workshops before going further north.

The apprentices were dispersed. Callum and Billy Gault and two others went on to complete their apprenticeships at St Rollox works in Glasgow. Here they were known as 'the country boys' and found life very different in a works with 3,000 staff. Others went to Inverurie works and Willie Peddie moved to the civil engineer's outdoor machinery department.

The Lochgorm buildings survived and were converted into the diesel depot which maintained the diesel locomotives that worked in the Highlands and later also the diesel multiple units that worked between Aberdeen and Inverness. The Gault cousins returned to work at the Inverness depot and Willie Gault was the depot engineer between 1987 and 1994.

Sir Peter Parker (right), the chairman of the British Railways Board, inspecting the new rotary snowblower at Inverness depot in 1981. Willie Gault (centre) was in charge of training drivers for the snowblower and was later to be depot engineer. Bob Taylor (left) was the area maintenance engineer. Willie's cousin, Callum Gault, was one of the drivers of the snowplough when it went on a long journey down to the south of England to clear snow on lines in the area. In 2004 the same snowblower was still maintained at Inverness depot, but was now owned by Network Rail and driven by a member of First Engineering's staff.

The depot staff in 2004

Some 46 years after my first visit to the Lochgorm site I returned to look at the work of Inverness depot on 9 September 2004 and was shown round by Derek Mackintosh, the depot production engineer. I was soon aware that Inverness was an extremely busy depot, but Derek explained that the workload had been greatly reduced in 1995 when its locomotives were transferred away following the introduction of diesel multiple units on all ScotRail services and the changes being brought in prior to privatisation. 26 staff were made redundant and it seemed likely that many more might follow.

Preparations for privatisation fortunately also opened up possibilities for filling the gap in the workload. The Anglo-Scottish Caledonian Sleeper services were transferred to

The former Lochgorm works building, which became the diesel depot in 1960. It is seen here in 2004 and is immediately recognisable from the previous photographs of steam locomotives being overhauled. On the right is one of the Inverness allocations of sleeping cars, and, on the left, a class 158 unit under repair, one of 23 based at Inverness.

ScotRail, who wished to maintain them within their own area, and the Inverness staff successfully put forward the proposal that they should be maintained at their depot.

In 2004 Inverness depot consisted of two buildings. The first was the original Lochgorm works where major repairs were being carried out to class 158 units and to sleeping cars. The second building was the carriage maintenance depot, on the opposite side of the Rose Street curve, which was opened in 1981. This building was a hive of activity during my visit as the sleeper vehicles were being cleaned inside and the berths prepared for the evening departure, in addition to the mechanical work being carried out.

The carriage maintenance building, opened in 1981, showing 158711 undergoing scheduled maintenance and the set of Caledonian Sleeper coaches which were being serviced after arriving from London that morning. Derek Mackintosh, the depot production engineer, examines the sleeping car. The depot maintains 53 sleeping cars, nine lounge coaches and 11 coaches for seated passengers.

The staff at the depot included several who had family connections with railways in the Highlands. Derek himself was the grandson of a locomotive driver from the LNER engine shed at Boat of Garten and nephew of a signalman at Dava. The shift supervisor during my visit was Callum Gault, who had been an apprentice at Lochgorm works at the time of my visit there in 1958. His son, Norman, was also employed as a shunter at the depot.

Callum Gault was working at a computer on my visit and this brought home to me the vast changes in working on the railways in the years since 1958, when the general conditions were not vastly different from a century before.

Another change is that on today's railways there are not the same reserves of either staff or stock that existed in former years. On 9 September 2004 Inverness depot was meeting all its targets for sleeper train vehicles, but was two below the target for its class

158 diesel multiple unit fleet, and a bus had taken the place of one of the Kyle of Lochalsh trains. The depot staff were trying to identify the intermittent fault on one of the problem 158s and an engineer was accompanying it on its next trip to Kyle.

One of the heartening features of my visit was to see that the depot was expanding, with construction taking place for new offices and larger staff facilities. The staff has grown to deal with the expanding workload and from a low point of 56 in 1995, increased to 81 in 2004, including an apprentice for the first time for several years.

A sleeping car protrudes from the carriage maintenance building. Carriages are also serviced at Wembley in London, Polmadie in Glasgow, Aberdeen and Fort William. Each set of eight coaches returns to Inverness every eight days. On the right are the two class 08 locomotives which ScotRail hires from RT Railtours for shunting the sleeping cars.

The increase in the staff and workload in Inverness depot is due to be followed in December 2005 by the introduction of the 'Invernet' rail commuter service from Kingussie to Inverness and from Tain to Inverness. This will result in further posts for drivers, conductors and maintenance staff being created.

CHAPTER 10

An Edwardian Railway Enthusiast in Nairn

Malcolm Blane

The coming of the railway had a major impact on Inverness. It also changed the fortunes of the other terminus of the first railway in the Highlands. In 1855 Nairn was a relatively sleepy county town with an adjacent fishertown. George Bain wrote in his *History of Nairnshire* in 1928:

Nairn station in 1913 with a Small Ben 4–4–0 about to leave with a train for Inverness. The station buildings date from 1885. Nairn was one of the first of several stations the HR rebuilt in the 1880s and 1890s, reflecting the town's importance on the system.

Few of the smaller towns of the north have benefited so much by the opening up of the country by railway communication as Nairn has done. Its prosperity dates from that development. A new direction was given to the enterprise of its citizens. It was then seen that the future progress of the town depended upon its development as a sea-bathing place... New streets have been formed and built upon. Numerous villas have sprung up in and around the town, and, with many comfortable and first class hotels and boarding houses, afford accommodation for visitors. A large indoor swimming bath and other bathing establishments have become attractions to the place.

Much of the development was due to the efforts of Dr James Grigor (1814–1886), who, in addition to his medical practice, promoted Nairn as a health resort because of its dry, mild climate, its sea air and fine beach. He was a leading light behind the building of the Royal Marine Hotel and the swimming baths. By the time of his death in 1886 Nairn was being called 'the Brighton of the North'.

It is not surprising that Dr Grigor was one of the provisional committee which promoted the Inverness & Nairn Railway in 1853, emphasising at a public meeting in Nairn that the proposed line would increase property values. The railway was built by the contractors Brassey and Falshaw and James Falshaw settled in the town during the building of the line. He stayed on after the line was opened in 1855 and became an ally of Grigor on the town council. He left Nairn in 1858, but later became a director of the Highland Railway; he was also chairman of the North British Railway and Lord Provost of Edinburgh.

The viaduct to the east of Nairn station, photographed soon after its construction in 1857. It was built by the Inverness and Aberdeen Junction Railway when it began to connect the Inverness and Nairn Railway to the Great North of Scotland Railway at Keith.

The hotels and houses that were built in Victorian Nairn created considerable traffic for the Highland Railway, as families came to Nairn at the beginning of the summer season and returned at the end. In *Nairn in Darkness and Light* David Thompson writes of how his great-uncle Sir Robert Findlay, the MP for Inverness Burghs and later Viscount Findlay, Lord Chancellor, travelled by train from Euston to Nairn in the 1900s with 40 servants.

4–4–0 14 *Ben Dearg* on a local train at Nairn shortly after it was built in 1900. In contrast, the basic third-class carriages behind are 30 to 40 years old. Some years later William Whitelaw, HR chairman and Nairn resident, said that such coaches were 'not good enough for carrying ordinary Christian Scotsmen over their line'.

Malcolm Blane's diaries 1901–2

The Blanes, Gilbert and Mabel and their son Malcolm and three daughters, were one of the families who came north each summer in the 1900s. The family had Scottish roots as Gilbert was a descendant of Sir Gilbert Blane of Ayrshire, a notable naval physician in the Napoleonic wars, while Mabel was a granddaughter of the 8th Earl of Galloway.

4–6–0 141 *Ballindalloch Castle* at Nairn in about 1910 with a train from the south. The traffic generated at Nairn was a major reason why most trains on the main line from Perth conveyed through coaches to Inverness via Forres after the direct Aviemore to Inverness line was opened in 1898. The water tower shown here was later removed.

Their main base, however, was in England. Gilbert Blane, a captain in the Scots Guards, owned the estate of Foliejon Park, Windsor, although the family lived in a rented house in London for much of the year.

Malcolm Blane was born in 1892 and his diaries written between the ages of nine and 12 (1901 to the beginning of 1905) survive. In them he recorded his railway journeys as well as how he spent his time. They not only help to provide a picture of railway travel in the 1900s, but they describe the life of a well-off Edwardian family, typical of many who travelled by the railway to Nairn each year. The Blanes also visited landed friends in England and travelled on the Continent. Their lifestyle is a contrast with that of most of the Highland Railway staff who, if they did take a holiday away from home, would stay with one of their relatives in Scotland.

The first 'Journey Book and Special Diary' of Malcolm Stewart Gilbert Blane contains less detail about Nairn than the following volumes. It starts in July 1901 with the journey from Windsor to Nairn, changing from Paddington to King's Cross station in London. Malcolm kept a log of this overnight journey, as he did for the return in October, part of which is shown below. The Blanes then travelled to Switzerland and France.

From 1902 we learn more about his journeys to and his time in Nairn. On 3 August 1902 the family left Gravesend in Kent and then took a cab from Charing Cross to King's Cross to catch the sleeper to Nairn. Malcolm's bed was beside the window and he recorded that he slept little on the journey because he was looking out all night. The train left London at 8.15pm, arriving at Nairn at 11.30am on 4 August, which would have been over an hour behind schedule. He was very impressed with the beauty of the Highland landscape and wrote 'If you go there mind you look at the scenery'.

Among the highlights of Malcolm's holiday in Nairn were the local Coronation procession (for Edward VII) on 9 August and

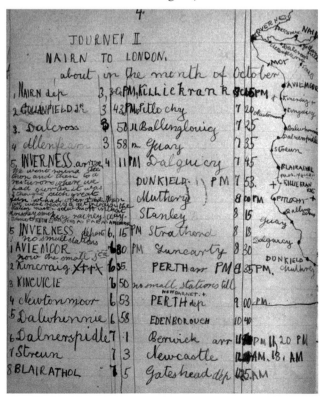

Page from Malcolm Blane's diary for October 1901, which records his journey from Nairn to London en route for France. Malcolm notes that it was only between Aviemore and Perth and New Barnet and London that the train stopped at 'small stations'. The spelling of the station names is rather erratic and suggests that someone may have been calling them out to him as the train stopped. Malcolm's spelling and writing improved as the years progressed.

4–4–0 11 *Ben Macdhui* at Boat of Garten with a local train in about 1918; the group includes the train crew and the stationmaster. The Small Ben class of locomotive was used on many of the passenger trains passing through Nairn. Malcolm records travelling behind *Ben Alisky* in 1902 when he would have been about the same age as the boy in the photograph.

the later 'MOST WONDERFUL SIGHT' of the 'Coronation Sinomate Graph' ('cinematograph'). Other events included a fathers v sons cricket match. Malcolm actually played for the fathers' team, whose best batsman was William Whitelaw, the chairman of the Highland Railway. Both Whitelaw and Robert Park, the HR's secretary and later general manager, made their homes in Nairn.

The diary describes several journeys, three of which involved cycling and railways. On 20 August 1902 Malcolm and his Canadian governess, Miss Jay, cycled from Nairn to Ardesier and then to Fort George, where a sailing boat operated a ferry to Fortrose in the Black Isle. On the return the boat had to be rowed because there was not enough wind and, probably because of this, they cycled as quickly as they could to Gollanfield Junction where they were going to catch the train for Nairn. It was pulling in from Inverness as they were arriving at the station and they got in with their bicycles 'frantically hot and tired' and without having time to buy tickets.

Malcolm and Miss Jay also cycled to Brodie Castle, catching the train back from Brodie to Nairn. On 9 September they made a return train journey to Allanfearn and cycled from there to see the Culloden Battlefield and Clava Cairns, with Malcolm also noting the 'very fine railway bridge' over the Nairn at Culloden. On arriving at Allanfearn he was not allowed to keep his ticket, but later found a pink one from Forres to Alves on the platform which he put in his railway ticket album.

The Blane family made trips by train to Elgin to see the cathedral and to Inverness to

Highland Railway postcard showing Cawdor Castle, which the Blane family visited while at Nairn in August 1902. In the 1900s the HR produced packs of six cards for various stations. The other cards in the Nairn pack included views of the town itself.

see the Highland Games before Malcolm had to leave Nairn on 20 September 1902. This was to begin his first term at Stonehouse preparatory school at Broadstairs; he had apparently previously been taught by governesses.

Whereas the journeys from London were direct to Nairn via Forres, return travel was via Inverness where the train to London was joined. At Inverness the Blanes had over 90 minutes to wait before catching the train to London so they took tea in the 'waiting restaurant'. They then went to their reserved carriage and settled in for the journey to King's Cross, receiving their dinner basket from the refreshment rooms at Kingussie. The diary records that Malcolm only slept for two hours between Blair Atholl and Dunfermline. The train arrived in King's Cross more than an hour and a half late; the journeys in the diary record poor timekeeping for various trains between Inverness and London and Nairn and Inverness.

1903–5 journeys

The diaries for 1903 contain details of railway journeys Malcolm Blane made in England during his school holidays. The Blane family spent five days with their relatives, the St Aubyn family in Cornwall, for the New Year's shooting in 1903: the total included 70 pheasants. They travelled to Bodmin Road and back by the Great Western Railway. In April 1903 they travelled by the London and South Western Railway and the Somerset and Dorset Joint Railway to Sturminster Newton to stay with Mr Pitt Rivers; the holiday pursuits here were more cultural, including a visit to General Pitt Rivers's museums.

On 8 July 1903 the Blanes again started their summer holiday by catching the night train north from King's Cross. One of the highlights of their time in the Highlands was a circular journey they made by the HR to Inverness, then by MacBrayne's steamer

230 NAIRN.

STATION HOTEL, Nairn.

FAMILIES, Tourists, and Commercial Gentlemen will find this first-class Hotel replete with every comfort and convenience, combined with strictly moderate charges.

Handsome Drawing Room, Coffee Room, Private Parlours, Commercial Room, Billiard Room, and Superior Bedrooms,
Furnished in first-class style and lighted throughout with Electric Light.
PARTIES BOARDED BY THE WEEK AND MONTH.   COOK'S COUPONS ACCEPTED.

Five minutes' walk from the Station and Ten minutes from the Golf Links.
'Bus and Hotel Boots awaits arrival of all Trains.
C. MACPHERSON, Lessee.

A 1901 advertisement for the Station Hotel in Nairn. The Blanes breakfasted here after their arrival from London in July 1903 as they did not have any food in the house they were renting. The advertisement refers to a horse-drawn bus and the 'Hotel Boots' meeting trains at Nairn station; many other hotels in the Highlands offered the same service.

through the Caledonian Canal to Banavie Pier, followed by a North British train to Fort William and another MacBraynes steamer to Oban. They stayed here for two nights and made a circular tour by steamer, horse-drawn coach and train to Glencoe. From Oban they travelled by Caledonian trains to Dunblane, Perth and then to Aberdeen and by Great North of Scotland train to Banchory. They then visited Malcolm's

The Blanes' circular tour from Nairn in August 1903. They travelled over four of the five Scottish railways as well as by David MacBrayne's steamers.

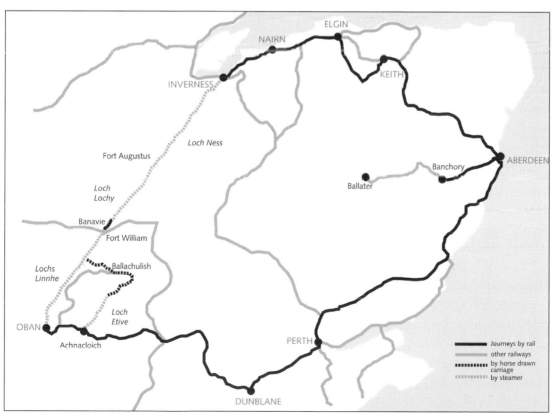

paternal grandmother. The family returned to Nairn over the Great North's inland route to Elgin and then over the Highland. The combination of train and steamer journeys was one which many Edwardian holidaymakers took advantage of in the Highlands.

A second journey made by Malcolm with his mother and Miss Jay was entirely over Highland rails. On 4 and 5 September they went by train to Kyle of Lochalsh, with Malcolm noting the scenic features en route; he also noted that the train arrived on time. A proposed visit to Skye was, however, abandoned because of rain. This was much to Malcolm's regret as the weather improved and the sun was shining when the train passed through Dingwall on the way back to Inverness and Nairn.

Kyle of Lochalsh station with the hills of Skye in the background. Malcolm was very disappointed not to be able to cross to Skye in August 1903. We know that he was later able to do this as a young man, as he is recorded as climbing the mountains of the island.

On 10 October 1903 Malcolm travelled back to school at Broadstairs, but this time by the West Coast route to Euston station in London. On the northwards journey on 31 July 1904 for the beginning of that year's summer holidays he was once again using the East Coast route.

Malcom planned to travel from Euston again on his journey back to Nairn on 22 December, but the fog was so bad that the night train to Inverness was cancelled. The fog still persisted the following evening, 23 December, and the night train eventually left over 75 minutes late with detonators going off to provide a warning of poor visibility.

The train was two hours late by the time it arrived at Perth, where the carriages for Inverness were detached from the main portion, which went on to Aberdeen. The scheduled Inverness connection had already left with the carriages from the East Coast route and it was first thought that the West Coast coaches would need to wait to be attached to the following train for Inverness. In the event, the Highland Railway decided

Perth General station in 1911. Malcolm Blane spent some time here on Christmas Eve 1904 before the Inverness section of the night train from Euston went forward as a special working. He records talking to the guard who then went on to Aberdeen with the main portion of the train from Euston. Malcolm then bought postcards from the bookstall in the background and ate breakfast out of a basket.

to provide a locomotive to take the three Euston carriages as a special train to Inverness. The train, which only stopped at Pitlochry, Kingussie and Aviemore, made up 45 minutes of lost time.

At Inverness Malcolm was met by some of his family and from there travelled to Nairn and to the house, Westfield, where they had stayed since 1902. It was Christmas Eve and the family unpacked 'the great wooden Christmas box'. The Christmas and New Year festivities in Nairn included a party given by William Whitelaw and his wife at their home, Monkland, where the entertainment included magic lantern slides.

Malcolm Blane 1913–1915

Malcolm Blane's surviving diaries cease at the beginning of 1905, but two diaries written by his younger sister, Sylvia, also survive. The interests of a 14 to 16-year-old girl were of course different from those of a 9 to 12-year-old boy and railways were not among them. The diaries do, however, tell us more about Malcolm, who was 20 when Sylvia's diaries start in 1913. The Blane family's Nairn home was now Seaforth in Seabank Road, although in 1914 they purchased Altann Donn on the fringes of the town, to which they later moved as their permanent home.

We also know from other sources that, after Stonehouse School, Malcolm had gone to Eton and then to Christ Church College, Oxford. In July 1914 he graduated with a degree in engineering and science. His interest in railways had clearly been maintained. He was a member of the Railway Club in London and after his graduation was writing books describing the development of the Highland Railway and Scottish railway engineering.

The booklet *Behind the Highland Engines* was one of the few published sources of information on the HR before World War One. It records the performance of locomotives on the different lines. Bob Ross is a driver whose name appears in the booklet as achieving good performances on Perth and Aberdeen trains through Nairn. 'Scrutator' was the *nom de plume* of the Revd A. Warburton.

While at university, Malcolm Blane had an extremely wide range of interests in addition to railways and engineering. He was president of the Oxford University French Club and travelled widely in France, Germany, Spain and Russia. He is recorded in *Celtic Monthly* for April 1915 as giving 'all his energy to the Scottish National Movement and the furthering of the Celtic Renaissance'. Malcolm was the founder of the University Gaelic Society and a member of the Inverness branch of An Comumn Gaidhealach.

On 2 January 1914 Malcom Blane was again to be found at a party at the Whitelaws' house in Nairn, as he had been nine years earlier, and six days later he was a guest at the Findlays' fancy dress party at Newton before returning to Oxford. He had one of his German friends with him. This encouraged Sylvia Blane to make plans to visit Germany that summer. Instead, in her diary of 4 August 1914, she recorded the outbreak of war.

Malcolm Blane had been a member of the Oxford University Cavalry Corps and then in 1914 joined the Cameron Highlanders. At first Sylvia Blane wrote in her diary that she was glad that, because her brother was not a regular soldier and was not very strong, he would not be sent to the front. This proved not to be the case and on 3 May 1915 Malcolm was suddenly summoned south from leave in Nairn. On 9 May the 5th Cameron Highlanders left for France and during 25–26 September 1915 Lieutenant Malcolm Blane, along with many other young men from the Highlands, was killed in action at the Battle of Loos.

The obituary for Malcolm Blane in *The Locomotive* for 15 October stated that it was largely due to his 'energetic assistance' that a series of articles on the Highland Railway and its locomotives was being published in the magazine. A surviving list he compiled of photographs in the Highland Railway board room in Inverness in March 1915 was probably for possible illustrations for the articles. While *The Locomotive* articles are

This portrait of Malcolm Blane accompanied the article about him in *The Celtic Monthly* for August 1915.

The Nairn war memorial. The list of names of those killed in World War One record the deaths of all three of William Whitelaw's sons, as well as that of Malcolm Blane.

important in being the first record of HR engines, one can only regret that he was never able to write the book on the Highland Railway. His achievements up to the age of 22 certainly merit the obituary in the *Inverness Courier*: 'By his death a life of great promise has been cut short.'

CHAPTER 11

The Highland Railway Recorded
W.E.C. Watkinson, Ian Scrimgeour, Gavin Wilson and James L. Stevenson

Many railway enthusiasts have recorded and researched the Highland Railway and Malcolm Blane, whose life was covered in the previous chapter, was one of the first. This chapter shows how four other enthusiasts recorded the Highland through their photographs.

W.E.C. Watkinson
W.E.C. (Ted) Watkinson (1910–1981), like Malcom Blane, became interested in the Highland Railway through summer holidays at Nairn. In the 1920s and early 1930s he photographed many trains on the Highland system.

Most of Ted Watkinson's life was spent in Worcestershire where he was a farmer, breeder and judge of pedigree Jersey and Aberdeen Angus cattle of international renown.

A northbound goods train near Dalnaspidal in September 1929. It is headed by LMS 0–6–0 4312 and is being banked by 4–4–0 14397 *Ben-y-Gloe*. These Midland Railway-designed 0–6–0s were among the first new engines introduced on the Highland section by the LMS.

In the 1960s, however, he renewed his connection with the Highlands, spending several holidays in Caithness and resuming photography in the region.

Ted Watkinson was closely involved with railway preservation, becoming the first president of the Scottish Railway Preservation Society and then a director and chairman of the Strathspey Railway which he greatly assisted. His name lives on in the W.E.C. Watkinson Trust, which now owns the HR brake van, Black Five 4–6–0 5025 and the four LMS coaches he preserved for the Strathspey Railway.

Clan Goods 4–6–0 17951 shunting cattle wagons at Kyle of Lochalsh in September 1929. These locomotives, displaced from the Perth to Inverness main line by new LMS locomotives, had begun to replace the Skye Bogie 4–4–0s (see page 84) which had formerly been used on the line. In the left foreground is a Highland Railway coach.

Preserved HR Jones Goods 4–6–0 103 at Nairn station on 23 August 1965, during the inaugural run of the trains from Inverness to Forres which marked the centenary of the formation of the Highland Railway. On the footplate are driver Edward Thorne (left) and fireman Andrew Robb (right).

A class 26 locomotive crosses the bridge near Achanalt station with an eastbound goods train from Kyle of Lochalsh to Inverness in August 1972.

LMS Black Five 4–6–0 5025 in 1970 after its repaint into LMS livery on the Keighley and Worth Valley Railway in 1970. The engine carries the livery it wore when working over the Highland line in 1934–5. Ted Watkinson purchased 5025 for use on the Strathspey Railway and it worked trains on the line after reopening from Aviemore to Boat of Garten in 1978. It also worked trains over the Kyle and Highland main lines in 1991 and 1992. In 2005 the W.E.C. Watkinson Trust is raising funds to restore the engine to working order.

Ian Scrimgeour

Ian Scrimgeour (1920–1999) was brought up in Dundee. However, his mother came from Tain and he spent many holidays at his grandparents' farm, north of Tain station. His grandfather, Colonel Fraser, could remember the line being built in the 1860s.

As a result of friendships he made with railway staff in the Tain area, Ian was allowed footplate trips and entry into Edderton, Fearn and other local signal cabins, where he was soon helping the signalmen in their operations. He recalled being told that a special

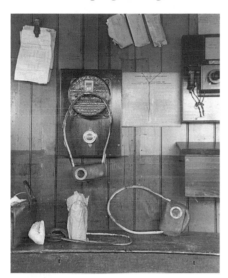

Dingwall North signal cabin in 1938 showing the Tyers Key instrument which controlled the operation of Dingwall to Strathpeffer branch trains which left the line to Kyle of Lochalsh at Fodderty junction. From 1936 a hand generator in the box worked the points at the junction and Fodderty Junction box was closed, although it was reopened from 1940 to 1944. The leather pouch with a wire hoop hanging on the instrument is for the Strathpeffer key. On the wall are various railway notices, while the signalman's meal rests on the bench below.

Dalanraoch signal cabin, on the double track section between Struan and Dalnaspidal, in July 1937. Ian recalled that the signalman had originally come from his own home city of Dundee. The box was moved to Edendon and a new Dalanraoch box opened further south to increase the capacity of the line during World War Two.

A northbound train headed by a Ben class 4–4–0 passes through Foulis crossing loop in 1935. The loop was installed in 1916 to increase the capacity of the line for the wartime traffic to Invergordon and Wick and Thurso. Foulis station is just visible in the background between the trees.

The signal cabin at Foulis crossing in 1935. The automatic tablet exchange apparatus, with its post fixed into a concrete base, is in the foreground. Crews of locomotives without automatic apparatus passed the tablet by hand to the signalman, who stood on the lower platform behind the light coloured cupboard.

The automatic tablet exchange apparatus in use at Edderton North cabin in 1937. Jones Goods 4–6–0 17917, on a northbound livestock special, is collecting the tablet for the single line section to Bonar Bridge.

train he had just signalled during World War Two was conveying Winston Churchill from a visit to Scapa Flow!

Ian's experiences in the Highlands in the 1930s and 1940s led to him becoming one of the earliest experts on HR signalling and operation. Although he emigrated to Canada in 1957, he frequently returned to Scotland and continued to pursue his interest in the Highland Railway. The photographs reflect his interest in signalling.

Gavin Wilson

Gavin Wilson, like his friend Ian Scrimgeour, attended Dundee High School. As in the case of many others, his interest in railways in the Highlands started after spending annual summer holidays there, first at Grantown-on-Spey and then at Carr Bridge.

After purchasing a camera in 1933 Gavin began taking photographs in the Strathspey area, extending the area he covered after the war. He summed up the appeal of photographing trains in the Highlands in steam days when he wrote:

> *What could be more pleasing than to stand among the heather in full bloom, the warm sun beating down, watching and hearing the distant exhaust coming closer and closer until just at that right moment releasing the shutter and knowing you have just the picture you want.*

In addition to taking some of the finest photographs of the Highland system, Gavin Wilson, who died in 1976, had an extensive HR 00 gauge model railway. The model railway room in his home at Wormit looked over the Tay Bridge.

B1 4–6–0 61292 pulls away from Perth with an Inverness train in July 1948. The work of this LNER engine was being compared with that of a Southern Railway West Country 4–6–2 and LMS Black Five 4–6–0 as part of a series of locomotive exchanges organised by the recently formed British Railways.

The view south from Culloden Moor station to the Nairn viaduct in September 1949. Gavin Wilson wrote that if you were known at a station you could 'hear interesting stories of happenings and amusing incidents'. This was the case at Culloden Moor, where in 1959 Gordon Reid, the stationmaster, told the author of several such incidents in his career. The original of this photograph was given by Gavin to Gordon Reid.

A Black Five 4–6–0 heads a southbound train across Murdoch Paterson's Culloden viaduct over the Nairn. The photograph was taken by Gavin Wilson from the south end of Culloden Moor station in about 1949.

A southbound sleeper train from Inverness, headed by a Black Five 4–6–0, approaches the Dulnain viaduct north of Carr Bridge station in about 1951. This was one of Gavin Wilson's favourite photographic locations when he was staying on holiday in Carr Bridge. He noted, however, that as the gradient was 1 in 60 downhill for southbound trains there was little or no smoke given off and the safety valves would be popping, as they are in this view.

The signalman (and dog) at Achnashellach in the 1930s. The informality of this photograph contrasts with the more formal portrait of the Carr Bridge staff below.

The station staff at Carr Bridge in about 1949. From left to right they are: Jimmy Grant, signalman, Donnie Gordon, stationmaster, Willie McInnis, porter, and Robert Sinclair, relief signalman from Forres.

James L. Stevenson

James Stevenson (1919–1997) spent 10 years of his boyhood in Inverness after his father was appointed agent of the Union Bank of Scotland in the Highland capital in 1922. He maintained his connection with the Highlands, frequently returning there for holidays. James developed a special interest in HR locomotives and photographed many of the survivors from the 1930s to the 1950s.

After wartime service James Stevenson joined the LMS in Scotland. His railway career saw him rise to become principal planning officer of the Scottish Region when he was responsible for developing many major projects. These included the reinstatement of the double track between Blair Atholl and Dalwhinnie.

The two-volume *Highland Railway Locomotives*, written jointly with the Revd John Cormack, is one of James Stevenson's contributions to the history of the HR. Another is the book on HR engine sheds which he co-authored. He also made his extensive photographic collection available to others writing on the Highland Railway.

14410 *Ben Dearg* stands at Aviemore on a September evening in 1947, preparing to work back to Forres. In the background are the high peaks of the Cairngorms. The Aviemore area was a part of the Highland Railway that James Stevenson knew particularly well.

The Highland station at Elgin looking towards Inverness in August 1950. Like many other HR stations at this period, it had hardly changed since the end of the 19th century.

0–4–4 T 55053 at St Rollox shed in July 1955, immediately after its overhaul at the adjacent works. This was the only Highland Railway locomotive to receive the British Railways passenger livery. One contemporary report said that this was possibly to mark the centenary of the Inverness & Nairn Railway in 1955. The engine returned to work the Dornoch branch, but was withdrawn only 18 months later after its leading axle broke.

B1 4–6–0 61532 halts at Nairn with an Aberdeen to Inverness train on a wet afternoon in August 1954.

26026 with a ballast train at Blair Atholl in July 1977. It is standing on the restored southbound line which has yet to be brought into use. The reinstatement of the double line to Dalwhinnie was one of the projects James Stevenson was involved with when he was principal planning officer for the Scottish Region.

Bibliography

Books and Articles

Avoch Heritage Association *Rosehaugh: A House of its Time* Avoch Heritage Association, 1996.

Bain, George *History of Nairnshire* Nairn Telegraph Office, 1928.

Bond, Roland *A Lifetime with Locomotives* Goose and Son, 1975.

Barron, Hugh (Ed.) *The Third Statistical Account of Scotland: The County of Inverness* Scottish Academic Press, 1985.

Coombs, Thomas 'Unsung Heroes of the Highland', *Highland Railway Journal* 1998.

Cormack, J.R.H. and J.L. Stevenson *Highland Railway Locomotives* 2 Vols, Railway Correspondence and Travel Society, 1988 and 1990.

Duncan, Willie 'A Look Back' *Permanent Way Institute Journal* 1999.

Ferguson, Niall 'Snow in the Highlands', *British Railway Journal* 1993.

Forbes, Alfred H. *Time Does Transfix: Recollections of a Forres Railwayman* Centre for Scottish Studies, 1997.

Glen, Ann *The Cairngorm Gateway* Scottish Cultural Press, 2002.

Glen, Ann 'On the Wagons', *Scots Magazine*, 2003.

Hamilton, J.A.B. *Britain's Railways in World War I* George Allen and Unwin, 1967.

Hawkins, Chris, George Reeve & James Stevenson *LMS Engine Sheds Volume Six: The Highland Railway* Irwell Press, 1989.

Hay, Jock 'Memories of Working Life: the Train Driver' *The Hub Inverness*, 2004.

Highland Railway Society, *Eastgate 11: A Brief History of the Inverness Site* Highland Railway Society, 2003.

Hunter, D.L.G. *The Highland Railway in Retrospect* Moorfoot Publishing, 1988.

Inverness Field Club *The Hub of the Highlands* Inverness Field Club, 1975.

J.E.C. (John Edgar Campbell), *The Iron Track Through the Highlands* Highland News, (about 1923).

Lambert, A.J. *Highland Railway Album* Ian Allan, 2 Vols, 1974 & 1978.

L. Linder *The Journals of Beatrix Potter from 1871 to 1897* Frederick Warne, 1962.

McConnell, David *Rails to Wick & Thurso* Dornoch Press, 1990.

McConnell, David *Rails to Kyle of Lochalsh* Oakwood Press, 1997.

McConnell, David 'The Carrbridge Disaster of 1914' *Backtrack*, 2000.

McConnell, David 'The Carrbridge Disaster of 1923' *Backtrack*, 2000.

MacDonald, Mairi A. *North's Great Enterprise* The Northern Chronicle, 1955.

MacDonald, Mairi A. *Highland Coronach* Paul Harris, 1984.

Mackay, W.J. *The Freemen of Inverness* The Highland Herald, 1975.

Mitchell, Joseph *Reminiscences of My Life in the Highlands* 2 Vols, David & Charles, 1971.

Newton, Norman S. *Inverness: Highland Town to Millennium City* Breedon Books, 2003.

Nock, O.S. *The Highland Railway* Ian Allan, 1965.

Price, Helen 'My Dad the Driver, *Steam World*, 2002.

Rae, Isobel and John Lawson *Doctor Grigor of Nairn* Dunlugas Publishing, 1994.

Ransom, P.J.C. *Snow Flood and Tempest* Ian Allan, 2001.

Sinclair, Neil T. *The Highland Main Line* Atlantic Publishing, 1998.

Smith, Martin *British Railway Bridges and Viaducts* Ian Allan, 1994.

Stirling, David 'The Highland Railway Staff in 1911' *Highland Railway Journal*, 1988.

Stirling, David 'Passing Trains, Passing Time' *Highland Railway Journal*, 2005.

Sutherland, Ian *The Wick and Lybster Light Railway* Ian Sutherland, 1987.

Tatlow, Joseph *Fifty Years of Railway Life* The Railway Gazette, 1920.

Tatlow, Peter *Highland Railway Miscellany* Oxford Publishing Company, 1985.

Thomas, John *The Skye Railway* David St John Thomas, 1990.

Turner, Barry *The Dornoch Light Railway* Barry Turner, 2002.

Thompson, David *Nairn in Darkness and Light* Arena, 1988.

Vallance, H.A. *The Highland Railway* House of Lochar, 1996.

Wilkie, Willie 'Death of a Loch, *Steam World*, 1994.

Wilkie, Willie 'Three Steps To Heaven' *Steam World*, 2001.

Wilkinson, Brian *The Hielan Line* Dornoch Press 1988.

Manuscript Sources

Highland Council Archives

Diary of William Smith, HCA/D345.

Diary of junior employee in civil engineer's office, Inverness, HCA/D410.

Diaries of Malcolm and Sylvia Blane HCA/D543.

Papers of Murdoch MacDonald HCA/D6.

National Archives of Scotland

Minute books of the Highland Railway BR/HR/1/1-13.

News Cutting books of the Highland Railway BR/HR/4/16 24.

Highland Railway Staff Records BR/HR/15/1-19.

Newspapers

Highland News
Inverness Courier
North Star and Farmers' Chronicle
Northern Chronicle
People's Journal
Perthshire Courier
Press and Journal
Scottish Highlander
Strathspey and Badenoch Herald

Index